Alison McNicol

Craft
BUSINESS
Heroes

"How We Did It"

30 Creative
Entrepreneurs
Share the Secrets
of their Success

A Kyle Craig Publication
www.kyle-craig.com

First published in 2012 by Kyle Craig Publishing

Text and illustration copyright © Alison McNicol

Design and illustration: Julie Anson

ISBN 978-1-908707-02-4

Contents

Sewing

Fashion/Accessories

Introduction

Welcome to Craft Business Heroes!

As a crafty entrepreneur myself, I love nothing more than reading about how others have launched and grown their businesses! Seeing how others turned a simple idea into a thriving business, and the challenges they faced and overcame along the way is hugely inspiring!

It was when writing my other book—*The Craft Business Handbook: The Essential Guide To Making Money from your Crafts and Handmade Products*—that I had the opportunity to interview lots of fellow crafty business people, which was a dream come true!

In fact, in the end I had so many great interviews—too many to fit in that book alone—that I decided to fill a whole book with interviews from some of the most interesting creative entrepreneurs out there.

Each of them have been so generous with their time and advice, and I hope you enjoying reading about their experiences and insider tips as much as I enjoyed speaking to them!

When I was starting out, I would have found a book like this a huge help—so I hope that, whatever stage of your creative business journey, you will find something to motivate and inspire you—and if you do go on to start your own creative business, I wish you the very best of luck!

Prepare to be inspired!!

Alison McNicol xx

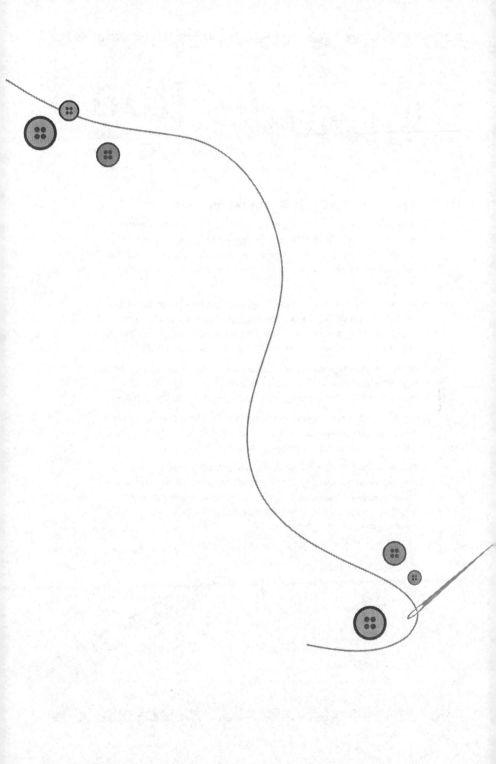

Jewelry

Pick Up Sticks
(jewelry company) *n.*

Name: **Sabrina Colson and Glena Henry**

Company Name: **Pick Up Sticks Jewelry Co. LLC.**

Founded in: **1999**

Location: **Clovis, New Mexico, USA**

No. of Employees: **4**

Website: **www.pickupsticks.net**

Cousins Glena and Sabrina grew up in Logan, a small town in rural New Mexico, population 500. The most entertaining activities in this rural area were swatting flies on their great grandmother's porch, building miniature houses out of rocks and bits of glass, and searching for the perfect smooth stone. Their great grandmother led them to explore a world of tiny hidden treasures, investigate abandoned houses and frontier dumps, while encouraging them to fill their pockets with sticks, stones, glass, feathers, and flowers.

Eventually, Sabrina and Glena each followed their own professional interests: Sabrina concentrated on art and graphic design, while Glena pursued business and education. Ultimately, the two combined their love of family heirlooms, antique finds, and time-worn treasures with their experience in the fields of art and business to start a company of their own, Pick Up Sticks Jewelry Co. LLC. What started as a new business venture has become a way for the cousins to revisit their past and those times spent with their great grandmother in a small town.

You each had your own successful careers before joining forces to launch Pick Up Sticks. Whose idea was it?

Glena had already opened a jewelry store, and I told her that I had an idea for how to combine photos and jewelry, and wanted to know if she would be willing to try to sell some of my pieces. She said yes, so I made about 20 photo charms; they got a lot of attention in her store. At the time, I was living in Arizona and Glena was living in New Mexico, and I heard about a wholesale show. We applied, were accepted, and we quickly realized that we had no idea what we were doing! We didn't know how to write an order, we used waitress ticket books. We had no displays, so we took antiques from my house. We didn't know industry terminology like minimum order, lead time, net 30, or exclusivity, so we had no rules. We wrote a couple of thousand dollars worth of orders, and thought, "we're rich!" But there was the heavy realization that we now had to make all of this jewelry ourselves! Let's just say that Glena and I stayed up until 3am for weeks, there was lots of vodka consumed, and we never got out of our pajamas!

When the business started, were you both still holding down regular jobs?

Yes, Glena was teaching school, and I was working on my student teaching.

Tell us a bit about Pick Up Sticks as it stands today—where are you based?

The studio, lead by Glena is in Clovis, New Mexico. I design remotely (with several visits a year) from Albuquerque, NM. We have 4 women who work flexible hours. I design the pieces myself (original collage using vintage images), with a ton of collaboration from Glena and the ladies in the studio. Our photo charms are framed outside of the country, then we assemble and ship from New Mexico.

Describe the early days of your business?

We were flying by the seat of our pants! The learning curve was like a roller-coaster ride. Traveling to cities where we had never been, going to market, it was fun, exciting and terrifying all at the same time!

How did you make ends meet in those early days, and how long did it take before you were turning a profit?

We were very conservative with supplies, and inventory. Never keeping more than we needed, but always having enough to fill orders. Cheap hotels, working out of our homes, small booths—we could take everything we needed to a trade show in just two suitcases. We were lucky, Pick Up Sticks never "operated in the red" and our only criterion for turning a profit was that we each wanted to at least make a teacher's salary. We accomplished that the first year, but we also only made this amount for several years after that.

At what stage in the business did you take on your first employee?

Right away, during the first year we needed help! We weren't sure we could afford it. But we knew that we wouldn't be able to fulfill our promises to our retailers if we didn't, and we knew that would not be a good business plan.

Manufacturing and sourcing—Do you make every single piece yourself, or employ help now? How has this changed from when you started out?

Again, we really lucked out on this one. A family member was able to put us in touch with the perfect manufacturer at the perfect time. We didn't have to research this one at all. With sourcing components, we had to have a lot of patience at first. Photo charms were being shipped to us with poor printing etc. There were a lot of quality control issues at first. Most of the issues were worked out in the first year. My advice here: just because a manufacturer doesn't get it exactly right the first time (or the second, or the third), don't give up. Have patience, but have a backup plan.

Trade Shows—an expensive, but necessary tool?

Oh yes. But this is how we built our business. No sales reps. We did it all ourselves. Plus, this was before the internet was such a marketing power for small businesses; we couldn't have built our business without wholesale trade show exposure. I'm not going to say, it was so small, but thank goodness that it was. We couldn't have handled a big show with a lot of orders at that time. OK. It was Oasis in Phoenix!

Buyers are at market to make important investment decisions, so provide them with helpful information about your line. These are professional, intelligent business people, and they don't need to be pressured. Do not "Sell"—EDUCATE.

When you are tempted to "sell", ask questions instead. What kind of a store do you have? Have you seen our line before? Do you carry anything similar? I know this seems like suicide, but encourage buyers to comparison shop. Ask them to let you know if they find a product that is similar to yours, that is better than yours. This will give you invaluable feedback on your pricing and quality.

Think of your booth backdrop as a billboard. Use beautiful graphics, showing your company name and clear product photographs. Use handouts sparingly, and think small. We give out a postcard with lovely product photography and contact information. We highlight our online catalog. Printing a full catalog is expensive, damn it. Plus, buyers do not want to carry a lot of bulky paperwork.

Have a current customer list; cut the dead wood out before every tradeshow. Serious buyers need to know if there is someone in their area that already carries your line.

Pick your booth location wisely. Research wholesale shows wisely as well, they are expensive, and a bad decision can break the bank. Do a mock booth set-up. Take photographs and take them to the show with you, this will save you a ton of set-up time. And get an "everything box": pens, stapler, tape, scissors, paper, business cards, rubber bands, etc. When you get to a show, it is like a ship-wreck—you will only have the items that you brought with you, so be prepared for everything and anything!

Use the lulls in traffic to network with other exhibitors, and for goodness sake be nice to them. Better yet, make friends with other exhibitors, and refer buyers back and forth. Other exhibitors have become our greatest mentors over the years.

If another exhibitor gets a customer in the booth, make yourself scarce. Exhibitors are at shows to service clients, they didn't come to chitchat with other exhibitors, unless time allows.

We make the joke that if the buyer is not in comfortable shoes, they're not a serious buyer; they are more likely someone who is at market to place personal orders.

> **You have a great website and sell directly to the public online. You're also stocked by hundreds of independent stores. Discuss the pros and cons of selling directly to the public, vs. wholesaling to retailers?**

Wholesale is the bread and butter of our company, and we believe always will be. The bricks and mortar stores that carry our line are the priority. Period. We made the decision a few months ago to start a retail website. We were sensitive about our pricing, and made it higher than our retailers would normally sell for. Yes, the retail margin is higher, but I caution anyone who has a large retail store base, because the retail website orders hardly justify the higher margin for us. The retail website simply does not produce much revenue. The collectors of Pick Up Sticks Jewelry need to touch, feel, play and experiment with different combinations of charms. They just can't do that online; they need to go to a store for that experience. We only provide a retail website to allow collectors a way to find a specific charm that a store may not have in stock.

> **How many and what sort of stores do you supply to?**

We now supply to around 900 in the US, a few hundred in Canada, and are soon to get a distributor in the UK.

> **How do you ensure you get paid by retailers on time to keep cash-flow moving etc?**

From day one, our policy has always been that we will not ship the order until it is paid for. And we do not charge a customer's credit card until the day the jewelry ships. The only exception to this policy is with much larger retail chains, catalogs, and museum stores. Oh yes, and the other exception is with retailers that we have a long history of successful business; we will allow them net 30 terms.

> **What do you wish you'd know when you started? Is there anything you would do differently?**

SHIP!!!!!!!!! Ship orders as fast as you can, fill the order complete. Communicate with your customers, pick up the phone and call them directly, the instant you foresee any problems or changes to the agreed upon plan.

Make it easy for customers to speak to you and encourage them to communicate with you. Give them your direct email address, let your staff give them your phone number if you are not at your desk, and return messages immediately. This is not a person with whom you will be in a short-term relationship; this is not a person you are "selling" to. This is a person who is your partner in business. Respect them, help them, listen to them, and make them happy that they have chosen your company.

I wish I would have known how hard it is to find a good sales representative—we currently don't use any. Same goes for showrooms. We currently have a wonderful distributor in Canada; a good relationship with a distributor can be a big financial benefit.

Best thing? Having a business partner that is freaking awesome! Glena and I compensate for each other's weaknesses, support each other's strengths, and a lot of the time, just stay out of each other's way so that we can do what we are best at. I know that is not something that "happened" to us, but it really is the best thing about Pick Up Sticks.

Worst thing? Doesn't even matter anymore, there is no advice that could have prevented the bad things that have happened, so it is irrelevant. Success is so sweet; I don't want to look back. Look ahead, work fast, learn from your mistakes, and SHIP!

Um, that information is in a hermetically sealed mayonnaise jar underneath the porch of Road to Ruin Bar in Logan New Mexico. No one knows the contents.

Alex Monroe

Name: **Alex Monroe**

Company Name: **Alex Monroe Ltd.**

Founded in: **1986**

Location: **London, UK**

No. of Employees: **15**

Website: **www.alexmonroe.com**

British jewelry designer Alex Monroe grew up in Suffolk surrounded by fields, rivers and the plants and creatures which inhabit them. He trained at Sir John Cass School Of Art in London, and uses nature to inspire his whimsical, intricately beautiful jewelry. Established in 1986, his core aspirations remain unchanged; to make great quality, wearable jewelry, which is originally designed and well priced.

Nature has always been Alex's greatest inspiration. Whether from travels in Pakistan, walks along the hedgerows of Suffolk or even the Tuscan hills, his designs always remain inherently English. Alex always makes the original by hand in sterling silver, which gives his work its distinctive signature of such exquisite detail. He uses his skills to craft jewelry that is slightly quirky, sometimes cute, but always very feminine. The jewelry is both pretty and humorous, but consistently wearable.

Japan has long been a important market for Alex Monroe, but the appeal of Alex Monroe jewelry can be seen all over the world, with a following of fans in Australia and Germany in particular. But back in the UK, there are now over 100 shops selling Alex Monroe jewelry. From high-end boutiques in London to sweet little shops in the Orkney Islands, the jewelry has won over fans young and old and become a firm favorite. Alex's designs are now the top-selling brand in many outlets, including Liberty of London.

Alex's distinctive designs have earned him many admirers in the press, as they are always a firm favourite with the girls working at the glossies! The now classic Bumblebee Necklace has graced the pages of *Vogue*, *Elle*, *Marie Claire*, *InStyle*, *Red*...the list goes on! The result of this is that the jewelry is now "must-have", and when Sophie Dahl was pictured wearing the Bee, stockists reported instant sell-outs, with boutiques across the country clamoring for Alex's classic designs. Despite this, the brand does not rely on celebrity 'endorsement', all clients are genuine fans—Sienna Miller, Emma Watson, Carey Mulligan and Thandie Newton, to name but a few!

In addition to producing four collections every year, Alex also embarks on numerous collaborative ventures, working with such luminaries as the Victoria & Albert Museum, who asked Alex to design a limited edition commemorative Locket. These diverse projects have also included an 18ct Gold Poppy for the British Legion, a 250th anniversary range for Kew Gardens, a bottle for the classic British perfumiers Penhaligon's and a set of sensual and erotic pieces for Coco De Mer. Alex's most recent project was working with Burt's Bees to create a limited edition Ring, and exclusive Necklace, both of which raised funds and awareness for the British Beekeepers Association.

In the middle of all this, Alex's original objectives stay true. Rather than compromise quality and have the jewelry produced in a factory, everything is still hand made in Alex's London studios by skilled crafts people.

In 2008 Alex was awarded the prestigious 'Designer of the Year' award at the UK Jewelry Awards, saying "His quality is perfect and his style is so consistent.' Alex also made the shortlist for this award in 2009 and 2010.

Tell us a bit about the early days? You studied at the Sir John Cass School Of Art in London—did you specialize in jewelry back then? After graduating what did you do?

When I was at university, I was much keener on silversmithing. I loved hand raising huge pots in copper and brass. It's an ancient organic technique which involves a hammer, a stake (steel former) and many, many hours of whacking! All the tutors were pushing a clean modern style so I did the opposite and hit things with hammers!

My course in those days was amazing. Four years long, with most of the third year out in industry. I worked in some amazing jobs in silversmiths and got all sorts of experience, but on leaving uni I couldn't afford the space or tools, so I reduced my scale and did it in jewelry. I soon realized I couldn't earn a living off gallery jewelry, so turned to an early love of mine; fashion. It worked, I got paid, and I loved it!

Describe the early days of your business—from having the initial idea to launching the business. Were you also juggling a job? Describe your goals back then? Did you even imagine the company would grow to this extent?

The early days were fun. I worked part time in a pizza restaurant in the evenings and ran my workshop during the day. I remember my first sale to a shop in Hampstead—four hollow silver axe earrings for £60! We all went down the pub and got thoroughly merry, and I had change left over! I'm afraid to admit that I was a precocious little twerp and believed I was going to change the world! I didn't get anywhere near that young man's ambitions. Thank heavens. Hopefully I've grown up a bit and am not quite as arrogant as I was!

I'm very pleased that I have been so lucky and my business has developed the way it has. Of course I have plenty more plans so we're not finished yet!

At what stage in the business did you take on your first employee—was it a big leap from making everything yourself to hiring others? How did you know you were ready and could afford it?

My mate Heather came and helped quite early on. It didn't seem like an employee. More like a mate helping out. I don't think it was a considered decision, I knew I could get the work if I wasn't tied to the bench, so Heather helped me to make and freed up a bit of time to visit shops and sell the jewelry.

Tell us a bit about where you work from these days?

I love my studio! It can get a bit busy these days, and a bit frantic. But when it's quiet, like in the evening or on a Saturday it's lovely. It smells nice, sounds nice and I've got all my best loved tools and knickknacks around me. It's like a favorite old pair of slippers.

Of course things have changed a bit—we might be 15 or more here, with 20 or so people working off site—we sell lots of jewelry all over the world so it's a global operation. I have lawyers, accountants, PR team, sales, managers and so on. But we have still remained the same at heart. Everybody is a friend. We still hand make everything here. I design and hand make each original. So it's essentially always been the same. Just more of us!

With all the day-to-day demands of running a business, how do you keep the creative juices flowing and find inspiration? How do you plan each new collection?

That's a problem. I have to change hats every few weeks. I'm just back from Japan being the face of the company (continuous interviews and receptions etc.). Now I have to put my designer's hat on and start with the new collections. Fear and panic are my main drivers!

Trade Fairs—An expensive, but necessary tool? Discuss.

We do London Fashion Week, Paris Fashion Week, Berlin and Tokyo. Occasionally we do something in the US. Yup, they're expensive all right. We get a lot of sales, just like in the old days, from good old visits with the stores. You can't beat a bit of leg work, and it's much more cost effective!

You have a great website and sell directly to the public online. You're also stocked by many independent stores. Discuss pros and cons of selling directly to the public, vs. wholesaling to retailers when the margins are so much lower?

At this stage I love selling direct. It gives us such valuable feedback and puts us in touch with our customer. I wouldn't want retailing to affect our wholesale business though, that is where our bread and butter has always come from. Margins are higher when you retail, but the amount of effort per sale is significantly higher.

You're very on the case with social networking—twittering, your blog, facebook page etc. Do you think it's important for your business to have such an online presence?

I love to blog, Emma who handles my PR is better at facebook, and Tom tweets. And we can all access each media so together we manage to keep in touch with our customers. It's really informative and productive so I wouldn't do without it!

The jewelry market is so competitive these days—what do you think you might do differently if you were starting out, compared to 20 years ago?

If I was starting out again I think I might go upmarket. A bit more lux. I love our price points because everyone can save up and be part of it. I hate snobbery or excluding people. But I reckon life might be a little smoother with higher price points. Not so much competing with mass producers and cheap imports.

With a London studio and team of staff, you've obviously grown considerably over the years. Overheads and cash-flow are one of the biggest challenges for a business owner. How do you ensure you get paid by retailers on time to keep cash-flow moving etc?

I'm really lucky with a brilliant team who stay on top of all these things. Over the years though I've had one philosophy; Take risks, be brave financially, but always make sure you can take the hit if it all goes wrong. We have had our share of difficulties but I've always been able to take the hit. Think of a business like a motor boat. You can go faster and faster, and create a bigger wake, but if you ever slow down your own wake might swamp you! (Did that make any sense?)

Your designs are so distinctive. Have you had any issues/experiences with copyright infringement, people stealing or copying your designs?

I've never copyrighted. I don't worry about it all too much. The trick is to keep evolving and move on. We have had a few of the big high street chains rip us off but it's straight to court and give them a nasty shock!

What's the best piece(s) of advice you've been given. What do you wish you'd know when you started? Any advice for others thinking of doing their own thing?

You only get out of something what you put in. I'm glad I didn't know anything when I started. Naivety and confidence is a great motivator. If I had known what I know now I might have thought twice!

My advice for others? Enjoy it! It's a wonderful world and can be so much fun. But for heaven's sake, if it's doing you in then go try something else. It's only jewelry after all!

And finally...what does the future hold for Alex Monroe...any exciting plans you'd like to share?

Too much excitement ahead for me to say. But how about this for a start; Our new building in London Bridge (being built specially for us)? A new web-site with loads of exciting projects for Christmas, and the new shop? And new collections, the USA, and so much more...Oh yes and I'm writing a book! Too many 'ands' I know, but you did ask!

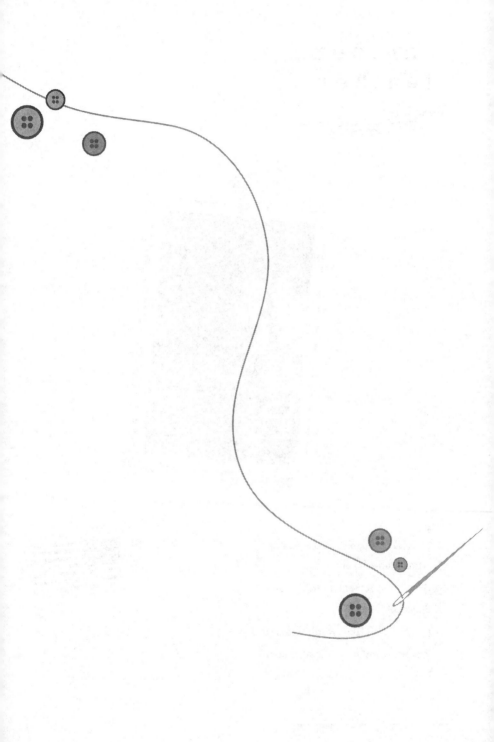

another feather

Name: **Hannah Ferrara**

Business: **Another Feather**

Founded in: **2009**

Location: **Asheville, North Carolina, USA**

Website: **www.anotherfeather.com**

Each piece of Another Feather jewelry is hand crafted by Hannah Ferrara in her quaint home studio in the Appalachian mountains of North Carolina. Her line includes one of a kind metal made jewelry, found object assemblages, and simple everyday adornments. She uses traditional metal smithing techniques and tools, and does all casting completely by hand. Each piece is slightly one of a kind, due to naturally unique imperfections, and evidence of the hand at work. Rustic and worn, all Hannah's jewelry is given special attention to detail, and is often made from objects found on travels, flea market excursions, and walks through the woods.

Tell us a bit about your design/career background what you did before you launched Another Feather?

I am primarily an artist (though at the moment I am also teaching art full time). I have a Studio art degree in both Metals/ Jewelry & Fibers. Before Another Feather I only made conceptual sculptural jewelry or large scale installation gallery work. Another Feather has opened up the design side of my work, and has given me a way to support myself financially with a production line, while still making my artwork. My business has also made a way for me to make my jewelry affordable for a younger low budget crowd, those (like myself) who maybe can't afford to buy the one of a kind art jewelry I make, but want to have something with the same style and ideas behind it.

Tell us a bit about Another Feather jewelry today—where are you based? Where do you design and make your pieces? How many and what sort of stores do you supply to?

Right now I am based out of the Appalachian Mountains in Asheville, North Carolina. I don't have any staff at the moment, I'm a one woman show (other than brainstorming session & organization help from my husband.)

I design and make all of my pieces in my small home studio—it can be super convenient but also a hindrance at times! It's hard to separate 'off' time and work time when you work at home. I am constantly going back to work, when I should be taking a break since everything is right there in my house.

At the moment I sell at 13 stores (5 of which are a chain that has 5 separate shops I supply to) and next year I am adding 5 more new shops to the line-up. I try to work with stores that have a common idea or aesthetic as my line. That said, a couple of the stores I work with might not fit with that idea, but are dependable and very successful at constantly moving my work.

Describe the early days of your business—from having the initial idea to launching the business. What were your aims for Another Feather when you launched?

Honestly I started Another Feather completely by accident. At the time I was a full time student (studying Studio Art), and had a part time job working in an art gallery. I had made a few samples that I enjoyed making, but took no time at all, as studies for bigger things I was working on in my Metals courses. Some local friends wanted to buy them, and suggested I open an Etsy shop. So I did, with five whole items in it (really rubbish items I might add!). They all sold in the following weeks, so I started to replenish with more samples. That summer, I had some free time, and started making some fun, affordable and wearable pieces and slowly adding them to my Etsy shop. Then overnight I starting having sales daily, and then a few weeks later I got 'The Call', From NBC's Today Show! They wanted to feature 10 pieces of my jewelry, which were to be overnighted to their NYC studio on their tab! I thought it was a joke, but I did it, and there my jewelry was two weeks later on national television (I didn't even have a television, so I caught it at a friend's house!). I was not prepared in the slightest to run a business—I had never even thought about it! I was so very lucky and blessed to be able to get on my feet so quickly and form a business, but it was also a hindrance since I had no time to plan for it or sit and think about what I really wanted to do!

Many designers find the business part of starting/running a business challenging. Did you have any help or advice when you started out? Did you do a business plan?

I'm not going to sugar coat it, the business side of things is pretty terrible and draining. If you can afford it I would say the most important thing to do is hire a trustworthy accountant. There's so many little financial/ tax/ self employment things that they inform and help you with, saving you money, stress, and time so that you can focus on making (cause that's really all we want to do right?). I am terrible at keeping books, and my goal for next year is to get good at it! I am just now getting around to doing a real business plan (I would recommend saving yourself a lot of pain, and doing this is the beginning). Luckily I have a very organized husband who forces me to think about business side of things. Also invest in some sort of financial organization software, so you can track your sales, supply costs, growth, and profit.

Online sales—You sell directly to the public on your lovely website, and also started out on Etsy. Did your own site cost a lot to design/build?

I sell through my own website (using embedded Big Cartel for now), on Etsy, and on Supermarket. I was very lucky to have a graphic designer offer to work for partial trade to design & build my website.

I can't really complain about Etsy, since that was how I first got a lot of attention and was 'found' in the beginning. That said, Etsy has changed a lot from when I first started using it. While still great, Etsy has become a bit overwhelming, and there is so much being sold on it, that your items can get lost under pages of search engines. For new entrepreneurs, I would definitely suggest opening an Etsy store in the beginning, but once you have a large following, slowly verge out on your own. I am in the process of doing that now. I still have an Etsy shop for convenience, but find it seems more efficient financially for me to sell on my own (those listing fees, and commission fees can really start to add up at the end of the month).

Also, Etsy used to have a very specific crowd of shoppers looking for well thought out and quality based items. Now with the growing popularity of the handmade marketplace (which is awesome!), you get all kinds of people shopping on Etsy. This is very positive but can also be hard when you have shoppers who are looking for the best deal, or for services similar to a corporation, and small business just can't afford to conduct themselves like a department store, or compete with those prices. By having your own website you are more likely to get a niche crowd who really appreciates your work and comes to your website to view your items and yours alone. I think boutiques, galleries, and other shops also appreciate when you have your own website with portfolio images, so that they can view your items in a professional matter.

Do you make every single piece yourself, or employ any help?

Yes I make every single piece by hand. Some production items I can churn out fairly quickly by using found objects and pre made parts and then assembling them, while other pieces where I make every bit by hand can be painstakingly slow to produce, but that's the process I love.

Selling to the public. Do you do many craft fairs? What are your experiences of these?

I'd say I do a fair amount of fairs. I don't tour and go to every single one like some other makers, but I try to do at least two per season. Every time I am preparing for a market, I ask myself "WHY AM I DOING THIS, IT'S HELL." But at the end of those fairs I always am so glad I did it, and realize the reasons why I continue to apply for more. They are exhausting, and hard work, (the preparation, and the day itself). But if you do the right ones, they are so rewarding in the end. It's wonderful to be able to watch people interact with your work in person, to hear feedback, and to meet your buyers face to face. It's also a wonderful time to hang out and network with other makers. I've also made many connections with stores, and gotten hefty wholesale orders from doing them, so the publicity (on the craft fair website) and getting yourself out there is reason enough to do a market even if you don't end up selling out.

My favorite fairs are: Renegade, Crafty Bastards, and The Big Crafty (in my home city), the Rock & Shop Market is another one of my local favorites and the first market I ever did, I still return each December for it.

I think putting plenty of time into planning your display is critical. Especially if you are doing one of the bigger well known fairs (you'll be competing against some display pros). Your items should be strong enough to speak for themselves, but you also want to think of your booth or tent as a real concrete shop. Wouldn't you be more drawn to a store which has an interesting display and has spent extra time creating a environment for their goods? The same goes for markets—people are probably more likely to go into your tent if something in your display catches their eye. I've found that's especially true for me as a jeweler, since many of these markets are loaded with other jewelry makers and we are all making such tiny things that can be swallowed under a tent. Creating an inviting and interesting space can really draw people in and showcase your style and product.

PR and Marketing—how do you reach customers? What seems to work for you?

I mostly use social networking to reach customers and keep them updated about new products. I blog about Another Feather and daily life, I have a business Facebook page, and a twitter account. This season I am going to try advertising on a couple of blogs for the first time. Every time I get written up in an article, featured in a shopping guide, or blogged about, I see a large increase in sales. Getting out there on the internet really is crucial to running a small business today. Social networking takes a ton of time, which is why I resisted so strongly in the beginning. At times I get really frustrated that I spend half of my day behind a computer updating my blog, Facebook, editing photos, and answering comments and emails, but I have actually witnessed a drop in sales when I do stop updating—proving it really is effective (though breaks away from all of this really are healthy every now and then). Ideally it would be awesome to hire some sort of PR assistant who could sit on the computer doing all these things, while I sat at my bench making things all day…one can dream!

Please describe the space you work from. How has this changed from when you started out? Any tips for those working from a space at home?

The space I make my work in is critical to my process. I surround my workspace with collected objects and different arrangements that inspire me whether I'm planning, designing, or making. I've always had some sort of workspace in my home, but while I was still in school I had access to some pretty incredible machinery and tools that I no longer have to use whenever I want. I have slowly built up my studio by buying one tool at a time, whenever I make a little extra money. This causes me to be a bit more creative and minimal when designing new pieces, and to use more hand tools when making. If possible try to have your home studio in a separate section of the house, not in the center. This might make it a little easier to switch mind sets when walking into your studio space, and walking into the kitchen to make lunch.

Is it really possible to make a decent living making and selling handmade jewelry? What would you say to others with this goal?

It's totally possible. You just have to realize it's going to be a slow process, and you are going to work harder than you've ever had to in your life. You will never sleep, and you will be your own everything at first (designer, accountant, maker, PR, photographer. Unless you can afford to hire these in the beginning! It's the most rewarding thing ever. I love knowing that I am financially self- sufficient from what I make. I think it may also depend on what you consider "a decent living", I'm a fairly minimal person, so it wasn't a problem for me. If you are going from a well-paid full time job, to starting your own business, it may be a different story. I also would not advise quitting your full time job until your business takes off. If you are smart with your money and your time you can be successful. One hard thing to consider is the fact that sales can fluctuate so quickly and dramatically. One month I might be making and shipping out orders all day, every day, and then go for a week where I sell only one thing. The main thing to remember is not to get discouraged, and to plan for this financially. If you have a low season, plan to use this time to come up with new designs and creations, and make sure when you have a booming month, to save up enough so that if the next is slow you are fine.

Words of wisdom. What's the best piece of advice you've been given?

I was advised to hire an accountant when I first started growing and tax time came around. That was the most valuable advice I have taken. I wish I would have had more time to do research on business practices before I started, instead of always playing catch up. I also wish I would have had a book like this one to see how other people did things!

Judith Brown Jewellery

Name: **Judith Brown**

Company Name: **Judith Brown Jewellery**

Founded in: **2004**

Location: **Wirral, UK**

Website: **www.judithbrownjewellery.co.uk**

Judith Brown began making jewelry in 2004. Her individual style has developed following her studies of Fashion and Textiles, particularly Embroidery at Manchester Metropolitan University. "I have always worked with stitch and wanted to develop a way of working that would highlight the stitch itself. Working with fine wire rather than thread has enabled me to create forms which are intricate and hold their form over time, yet are still seemingly delicate."

Judith exhibits regularly and sells through independent shops, galleries and specialist markets and fairs. She also runs workshops.

Tell us a bit about what you did before you launched your own jewelry line?

I studied GCSE and A level art, foundation art, then a degree in Embroidery from Manchester Metropolitan University, followed by a gap of about 10 years when I didn't do anything very creative. I trained to teach English as a foreign language and spent 5 years living and working in Italy. When I came home I discovered wire and haven't stopped since. Before I started making again at that point I had assumed that perhaps my creative days had passed, so starting making jewelry was a revelation!

Describe the very early days—from having the initial idea to launching the business?

The very early days were about figuring out what I should make with the technique I had developed with wire, and whether I wanted to make just jewelry or other larger wire items. I also had to work out what sells and what prices people were willing to pay. Then I had to find a market for the work, through local events and galleries. Looking back, the first 2 years or so were about doing this, and my business has grown very slowly and organically since then.

I have juggled the business and teaching work since the beginning, which is common for many makers. It is also probably why it has developed slowly. However in the last 2 years I have done less and less teaching work and the ideal would be to be able to concentrate entirely on the jewelry business…maybe next year?!

Where do you design and make your pieces? Please describe your workspace? How does this differ from when you started out?

I work from home and have a studio upstairs, which is full of things—from boxes of buttons, hooks and eyes and other haberdashery to a computer, to some of the display equipment I use when I do events. There are posters on the wall for some of the events I have taken part in. I will confess that it's not tidy, but I think that's an occupational hazard of being creative and running your own business, so many things to do and lots of things to make!

Do you make every single piece yourself, or employ help now?

I make everything myself. I don't employ staff as yet, though I have just started hiring professional support with the PR and promotion side of things, and the next thing I would like is professional help with my accounts!

I supply at the moment around 40-45 outlets. These are mostly small independent gift shops or boutiques, craft and art galleries, and also some museum shops and one or two online shops or marketplace style sites.

Do you show at any Trade Fairs?

My first trade fair was the British Craft Trade Fair (BCTF) in Harrogate. It was a really scary experience, so much to think about—your stand design, your ranges, your prices and promotional materials, where to stay, will you get any/too many orders, how to talk to customers—and will it all fit in the car?! But in fact it was a great experience! I met makers who are real friends now and I did get orders too! (Though on one order I wrote I used the wrong side of the carbon paper so that when I came to give a copy to the customer it was blank—very embarrassing!) I still do BCTF now, there is always a buzz about the show, it's really friendly and you are competing with other makers like you, rather than big businesses so it's not too intimidating. I think you have to keep going to the same events, one year is not usually enough. In the last 2 years I have orders from businesses that took my card 4 or 5 years ago, and have finally ordered. If you want to do exhibitions through galleries BCTF is a good event to do.

This year I also did Top Drawer Spring in London, and have rebooked for next year. Unlike BCTF the products sold don't have to be handmade in Britain, so you can be competing with really big businesses selling products made in China. It is a different kettle of fish altogether. Although I ended up with some good new customers and meeting some great other makers, at the start I was terrified! Even though I was confident in my work, there was just something overwhelming about the size of the event. When I walked in off the train with my little suitcase to set up my 2x1m stand and I walked past all these enormous 24m^2 stands, and I felt very small indeed and it kind of shook my confidence a bit too. The high for this show was securing an order from the British Museum and orders from abroad.

Although they can be scary I think you need to do them to get feedback from customers and make new contacts, and for me that moment when I have put the last price label on and I can step back and look at my jewelry displayed how I want it to be gives me a buzz.

Selling to the public. You do plenty of craft fairs and wedding shows? What are your experiences of these?

I like doing fairs. When you work on your own it's a chance to get out there and show your work and meet people, and I do get some fantastic reactions to my work—from incredulity to delight. One customer at a recent event said, "It's just so wonderful I could curtsey in front of you!" Now that can't fail to make you smile! At first I didn't know how to talk to customers, but it is something that you can learn. Just saying hello is enough to gauge a person's interest, if they are interested in knowing more you can learn to read their body language.

Highs are when you have great reactions to your work, and of course good sales, or it might be a new friend made in another maker. Lows are not selling anything, and starting to question everything from your display to the work itself, feeling frustrated and fed up—but then there's usually nice cake at these events which can help at these moments!

Fairs are time consuming and can be expensive, so it's worth planning out your year ahead, so you don't spend too many weekends away, or have too many events close together. My tip would be if you have done a weekend event that finishes on a Sunday and you have to pack up, and have a long drive ahead of you, I think it's worth staying the extra night if you can, much safer and much less stressful. I've driven home in foul weather, hit traffic and diversions and been delayed then had to teach the next day, which was really hard.

As to which fairs to do, there are lots out there, which will suit different makers and work. Many big events you have to apply for more than 6 months in advance, so that's why researching and planning ahead is important. I did lots of small events and local events which weren't expensive while I was still developing my ranges and these can be a good way to start, even if sales are not fantastic, it gives the deadline of getting a display and products together.

Pricing—how did you get the retail price right for your pieces? With the wholesale margins so much tighter then retailing, how do you ensure there's enough profit?

When designing a piece I think about how much it can be retailed for realistically and then work back from there. Time is the biggest consideration, followed by materials.

You have a great website and sell directly to the public online. You're also stocked by many independent stores. Discuss pros and cons of selling directly to the public, vs. wholesaling?

Selling direct to the customer gives you more of a buzz, you get that personal interaction with the person buying your jewelry, and you can find out why they like it and learn from that too. You do make more money, but then you have other costs to consider, petrol, stand costs, accommodation costs etc. If you do a fair you need to build up quite a lot of stock with no guarantee of sale.

Selling wholesale can be good because you get an order, make it, send it and get paid, without any additional costs, good customers can reorder regularly which is good. However, you still need to consider the time for typing invoices, labelling and packing up jewelry, and, unfortunately, chasing those who are very slow at paying their invoices, which can cause cash flow problems. Also it's harder to get feedback from the end customer on your product, and you don't have any control over how it is displayed.

PR and Marketing—how do you reach customers? What seems to work for you?

An email newsletter is useful, as are facebook, twitter and my blog. Up until now I think I have been lucky to have been approached by the magazines that I have been included in, though I have written press releases on occasion, and now I am getting professional help with PR. It is hard to measure magazine advertising. I had an advert in Crafts earlier this year and have been busy this year, but whether the two are directly connected I'm not convinced!

With all the day-to-day demands of running your own business, how do you keep the creative juices flowing? How do you find inspiration and plan each collection?

I will usually have an idea and then be too busy to do anything about it for a few months! Sometimes a customer will want something slightly different from how I usually do it and that can spark new designs, or even a new collection. I get ideas from the objects that I use in my jewelry, such as the hooks and eyes or old lace, and try to use my wire stitching technique to compliment their properties.

What's the best piece of advice you've been given. Any advice for others thinking of doing their own thing?

My work and my business have grown organically, not really to any strict structure, which it now needs. Looking back, having a set plan at the start might have helped my business to come together sooner, but then I also had a lot to learn before I was ready for this, both personally and creatively. So if you are the sort of person who isn't intimidated by business plans and actually writing down aims, then I think this is a good route, though it wasn't right for me.

Talk to other makers with more experience who you get along with, they can really help you, but remember networking is a two way thing and don't take it for granted that they will give you chapter and verse on every aspect of their business—they've worked really hard to get where they are!

There is a lot more to being a designer maker than just making, and you will spend a lot of your time doing other things—answering emails, paper work, invoicing, ordering supplies, doing applications for events, taking and editing photos of your work, designing brochures, prices lists and postcards and packaging, writing press releases, tweeting blogging, pricing, labeling, driving—in fact sometimes I do have to make time to make!

And finally...what does the future hold for Judith Brown Jewelry...any exciting plans you'd like to share?

I have a website redesign planned in the next few months so that I can improve online sales. I'm also hoping to add in another trade fair next year, and promote my new bridal range of designs, and I'd like to be in a position to be working full time exclusively on my jewelry!

JEWELS & GIFTS

Name: **Marcia Maizel-Clarke**

Company Name: **Dogeared Jewels and Gifts**

Founded in: **1991**

Location: **Culver City, California, USA**

No. of Employees: **90**

Website: **www.dogeared.com**

Dogeared Jewels and Gifts have been hand crafted in California since 1991, when designer Marcia Maizel-Clarke recognized the need for jewelry that speaks. Their style is modern and versatile, inspired by California's free-spirited, natural beauty. Designs range from subtle classics to eclectic, unexpected statements, all designed in the spirit of love, kindness, and consciousness.

Dogeared jewelry is now stocked in thousands of stores worldwide, and each and every jewel is handmade in the USA, collectable, and one of a kind.

Tell us a bit about the early days? Were you working a job when you started out? What were your aims for your "creative business" at that point? Did you even imagine you would reach this level of success?

We never imagined it would be this big, but once it all started happening it felt extremely natural, so we went with it! That's just how it's always been for us...

I started out making eyeglass chains because I loved putting the different combinations of beads together, making something functional into something beautiful, and just creating something with my hands. I didn't make them to sell them, but people wanted to buy them... so it just sort of happened on its own. Then I started making jewelry that I wanted to wear and give to my friends, and the same thing happened! People wanted to buy it, so I let them, and Dogeared was born!

Once we realized this was a business—and it took a few years—we just did one thing at a time. We needed a name, we needed a studio, we needed more people to do more things... Dogeared didn't start out with a specific big picture goal, but we did have a vision of what kind of company it would be. The way we live as people is the way we do business, so our ultimate goal has been to keep the Karma good. We sourced Earth friendly materials, formed partnerships with nonprofits to give back, and kept everything handmade in the USA to create jobs in our community and support other American businesses. We stayed true to ourselves as we got bigger... I think that's where a lot of people go wrong, by compromising on quality and ideals in favor of building a business. But for Dogeared, I think that's where we got it right, and why we're successful. It pays off in the end!

Do you remember your first sale, or very first wholesale order?

Our first big sale was to Macy's. I had been a buyer there, and so when we felt Dogeared was ready I scheduled a meeting with my old colleague, and she bought for 10 stores. I remember feeling so excited... Dogeared had arrived in a major department store! We were always committed not to grow until we were ready, which kept our expenses in check. I balanced believing in Dogeared and what this business could become, with thinking and spending practically.

At what stage in the business did you take on your first employee?

We hired our first employee after we'd been in business for about a year. We just needed more hands! Dogeared was still very small, but we needed help! So we hired a woman through the work program at a local non-profit. We helped her make ends meet and learn some new skills, and she helped us juggle all the aspects of being a new business.

Tell us a bit about Dogeared Jewels and Gifts as it looks today, 20 years on! How many stores and how many countries do you sell in? How many staff do you employ? Describe your Culver City HQ—what happens there?

Dogeared is sold in thousands of stores in countries around the world, from major department stores like Bloomingdale's and Nordstrom to small boutiques and specialty stores. Our team has grown to 90 people, and everything happens in the same building- design, production, shipping, sales, accounting, marketing... Everything!

We really try to foster team spirit and a creative, collaborative environment where everyone's ideas are valued and heard. We've discovered some really talented people who came in looking for one job and ended up doing something completely different... One of our designers started out as a pieceworker, our copywriter used to be our production coordinator, and our design manager started out as an assistant. We have an amazing team, and that is such a gift- everyone contributes something special.

Sourcing and Production—With so many stores to supply to, and so many great designs, that's a lot of jewelry to make!

We still make everything in-house at our southern California studio. There are just a lot more people doing it! We grow as we need to grow. We have a rhythm to what we do, so we know when we need more people to make it all happen.

We're lucky to have amazing suppliers...for everything from chain to gemstones to findings. We are passionate about keeping everything local, so Dogeared deals only with U.S. based companies. That is by no means the cheapest route, but it's what's right for Dogeared. I think the people we work with appreciate that...Our vendors have a lot of competition from other countries. For example, the company that makes our boxes is the only place in the U.S. that makes the kind of boxes we need! So since they know Dogeared is committed to supporting other American businesses, they value our business even more.

Our partnerships are hugely important to us. We have worked with some of the same local vendors, artists and suppliers for many years, and that makes a huge difference—both for us and for them. Working with the same people, we build relationships and trust. They know we are trustworthy and will pay them for their work, we know they will uphold our standards of quality and our commitment to be Earth friendly. When you find the right people to work with, keep working with them. They're a part of your team!

How long had you been in business before you were ready to wholesale? Any tips for those considering wholesaling and doing their first trade show?

We were in business at least a year when we wrote our first wholesale order to Macy's, and we did our first trade show after about two years. It was an amazing experience... We had so much fun creating our booth, and really loved exploring the trade show world. We learned so much and met so many fellow designers and business people!

My trade show advice: Bring a gift! Offering something to the buyers is like having your sales team in 1,000 places at once. If it's something interesting, it creates a buzz around your booth. Also, remember that it's YOUR showroom. Style your booth in a way that communicates the brand identity, and bring everything. If they can't see it, they won't buy it. Catalogs are great, but seeing everything live and in person is what the shows are all about. Last but not least, make sure your sales people are like walking, talking encyclopedias about your products and your brand. They should be ready to communicate the company profile and know the full story about what's new and what the bestsellers are, as well as what things are made of, how to merchandise, etc.

You have a great website and sell directly to the public. Does a business need to wholesale to succeed?

I think a designer can create a business selling directly to the public, but there are a lot of stars that have to align in order for the brand to thrive. Celebrities, bloggers, and the press need to know who you are and tell your story to the people who will become your customers. By having a wholesale business, you're working within a network—retailers have customers in their stores every day, meaning that people see your designs every day. I think if you want to go really big you need wholesale to succeed, but it's not mandatory, and it's not for everyone.

I love Dogeared.com! Our line is so huge— there is no store on Earth that carries everything (you would need an entire store!) so having this presence online is really great for people who love Dogeared and want to see all of it. It's also a place where our team gets to be wildly creative in the way we show our product and talk to our customers. Instead of relying on a retailer to merchandize our jewelry, we get to do it ourselves. It's our playground!

The jewelry market is so competitive these days—what do you think you might do differently if you were starting out, compared to 20 years ago?

I wouldn't change the way we did things. Even things that don't work perfectly are meant to be... That's how we learn. I would give the same advice today as I would have 20 years ago: Just begin! Follow your heart and it will lead you towards what you're supposed to do.

We're going to keep having fun, doing good in the world, and expanding our circle of good Karma... We're just getting started!

20 Years of Dogeared !

1991	Handmade beaded eyeglass chains sold at Rose Bowl Flea Market, Pasadena, CA.
1992	First necklaces are made—Dogeared is born!
1995	Dogeared moves out of the house and into its new space in Venice, California
1996	Introduction of World Jewelry
2000	First wholesale catalog published
2001	Created first House Blessing
2003	Introduction of Make a Wish, wishbone necklace
2005	Introduction of Karma necklace
2007	Outgrew Venice studio, moved to new Culver City office
2008	Dogeared blog goes live
2010	Dogeared Bridal unveiled. Sex & The City and Eat, Pray, Love jewelry debut.
2011	20 years of Dogeared!! What next?

Marcia Maizel-Clarke's
Top Ten Tips for Creative Business Success

1) Keep it simple. Simple is hard to do well, but simple is memorable.

2) Have retail experience. Know what you're getting into! Learn what matters to retailers, how salespeople think and how shoppers shop.

3) Build a great team. Ideas come from everywhere when you surround yourself with the right people. Of course we look at resumes, but we make decisions based on a person's energy and attitude. You can teach people how to make a spreadsheet, but you can't teach them how to be a rock star at their job.

4) Quality is queen. Never compromise the craftsmanship and integrity of what you create.

5) Get Press! All press is good press. Create your brand story, find your brand voice, and reach out to celebrities, stylists and bloggers to tell them about it. Make sure someone is always ready to answer all press inquiries and provide images and information about your brand.

6) Make sure everything you want to sell is photogenic. Something can be lovely in person and look horrible in photos...making it a hard sell in the age of catalogs, email blasts and websites.

7) Work organically. If something is not looking right or making sense, it's probably for a reason. When it's right, it's right, and you'll know!

8) Think like a business person, act like an artist. Know how to figure out costing and maintain a good profit margin without compromising your creative vision, quality or brand identity.

9) Try new things. Know what you do best and keep doing it, but explore your options! In the past, Dogeared has made candles, journals, ornaments and underwear... Some ideas are more successful than others, but it definitely keeps the creative juices flowing!

10) Believe. Believe, believe, believe, believe. If you don't have faith in what you're doing, no one else will.

Kate Hamilton-Hunter Studio

Name: **Kate Hamilton-Hunter**

Company Name: **Kate Hamilton Hunter Studio**

Founded in: **2004**

Location: **North Wales, UK**

No. of Employees: **8**

Website: **www.katehh.co.uk**

Kate Hamilton-Hunter began her working life as a seamstress, specialising in bespoke bridal gowns. After four years in college and 5 years teaching Art & Design, a career change was brought about by a discovery of metal. Starting with aluminium, copper and brass, Kate soon discovered a new material to make jewelry from—recycled and reclaimed biscuit tins. Now officially a biscuit tin expert, Kate designs most of the jewelry she sells and makes an Antique range to order, and is developing a gallery range of one-off pieces.

Tell us a bit more about your design/career background what you did before you launched the business?

When I went back to college, I trained in embroidery, textiles and design, planning to expand my bridal collection with embroidery designs. However, I discovered a whole world of design development and techniques that took me away from my sewing machine and into metalwork. My final Textiles collection was constructed entirely from metal pieces, pieced and assembled using textile techniques. After four years in further education, I then taught Design & Textiles at two local colleges, teaching for 5 years whilst developing my own style, eventually finding my niche in jewelry. In 2004, I opened a craft unit at Bodnant Gardens, North Wales, making and selling jewelry on-site. I then branched out into selling to trade by exhibiting at my first trade show in 2005. I closed the craft shop after three years to concentrate on selling to galleries, shops and boutiques.

Tell us a bit about Kate Hamilton Hunter Studio today?

My studio is next to the sea on the coast of North Wales. I employ two admin staff and six jewelry-makers. I mainly design here in the workshop but have to wait until everyone's gone home or come in on a Saturday! I have to let one idea flow into the next and I can't concentrate if I get interrupted all the time! I also keep a sketchbook going and keep my camera handy too, as you never know when you'll see something inspiring. The jewelry-makers make the orders from my masters. I still make some of the more one-off pieces and silver pieces, and I think it's important to do that to keep in touch with the making process. We supply all sorts of stores, mainly small independents who want to offer the public beautiful, unusual, British-made products.

Describe the early days of your business—from having the initial idea to launching the business. Were you also juggling a job?

I was teaching while I experimented with different products. I was a member of a Textiles group who exhibited regularly and that was a great way to test my designs out on the public. When I opened the craft shop in 2004, I initially sold lots of metal designs in my craft unit, framed work, clocks and sculptures made by myself and other metal designers.

Did you work from home at first? Was taking on a studio space a huge leap of faith?

I am one of those people who started on my kitchen table. I then used a converted stable at my parent's house for free—Thanks Mum & Dad! And then rented the craft unit at Bodnant Gardens. We moved from that to a workshop. I think the most important thing is to grow slow and steady. When I've tried to leap ahead of myself, I've always come unstuck and had to have rein myself in.

Your pieces are so eco-friendly. Working with recycled biscuit tins is such a unique idea. Where do you find inspiration for each new collection?

When it comes to designing time, I look through my sketchbooks for shapes and ideas that can be expanded into one or more pieces (that's why it's so invaluable to keep a sketchbook going) and I look for new components, e.g. we recently converted to using all Swarovski crystals in our designs. I then think about the season I'm going into; Spring, Summer, Christmas, as it's important that the collection is relevant to the buying public. I also push myself to expand my own skills and recently trained in silversmithing so that gives me more scope in designing new work. Then I start chopping up tins and see what happens!

You now employ help to make each piece by hand, rather than make it all yourself. How has this changed from when you started out?

As I'm a designer, I realized very early on that I take too long making things as I fuss too much over which bit of tin to use and I get bored easily! So, I employed makers from the start. It's also astounding how much time it takes to run the business. I have weeks when I don't make any jewelry just because there is so much else to do.

When you first started, how did you find the right suppliers for all your findings etc? Any advice on sourcing parts and dealing with suppliers?

The thing to do here is to shop around for the best components and the best price, and you'll find you buy from a few different places. Then, if one supplier lets you down, you've already got an account somewhere else and can switch over to them for a while. The trade shows are a good place to find suppliers (but check they're based in the your country or you'll have import taxes etc to pay) or, I find asking other makers is a reliable way of finding good suppliers.

What have been your experiences of doing Trade Fairs?

Trade fairs are definitely the way to find trade buyers, but do your research. My worst show was one that I didn't visit first and it was totally the wrong environment for my jewelry. So, always go as a visitor and don't be afraid to chat to other exhibitors for advice. I don't mind if someone says 'I'm thinking of doing this show,

how's it been for you?' They are quite stressful in the preparation, travelling and set-up but when you come back with a full order book and you've got some lovely new customers, it's so worth it! I don't like the huge shows at the Birmingham NEC, I think they're too big and impersonal so I stick to Top Drawer London, Harrogate Home & Gift and Pulse. I also exhibit at the British Craft Trade Fair in Harrogate in April and think that's the best one to start at for a small company making hand-made products. Lots of gallery-owners attend and small independent shops who are looking for people like you to find before everyone else does!

You have a great website and sell directly to the public online. You also wholesale to retailers. For new designers starting out, please discuss pros and cons of selling directly to the public vs. wholesaling to retailers?

Our main business now is to the trade, and our website has a trade site hidden behind the retail site, so we use it to take orders from shops as well as the public. The main benefit of selling to trade is that you can get your product in front of so many people who you would never reach on your own. Imagine how many people see our jewelry in 450 shops compared to how many people would see if I had one shop in my local town!

The downside of course is the price; you have to sell your product for less than half the price you'd sell to a retail customer. But, actually you can make more money by selling to trade. All you have to get your head around is making things quicker using batch production methods, buying components in bulk so you get them cheaper and renting a workshop is miles cheaper than renting a shop in a great location. Your wholesale price has to cover all your costs and then it's doubled up + VAT to get the retail price. Then, if you also sell to retail customers, you're quids in!

Any tips on finding a balance between work and family life?

I'm a single Mum with four boys, but I get a few days off a week from being a Mum as they stay over with Daddy. I use this time to get in a few extra hours!

You have to find a balance between home and work, or you will suffer from stress and you must remember, you didn't start a business because you wanted to feel stressed and tired all the time!! It's very tempting to work all hours to get everything done and there are times when you just have to do that, but keep a check on that and take some time out. I have found going to my yoga class every Wednesday has been my rock, it reminds me every week to take care of myself and that some things are more important than work!

What's the best piece of business advice you've been given?

Be realistic about your strengths and weaknesses—pay people to do the things you're rubbish at! Don't kid yourself that you'll do your books once a week—employ a book-keeper! That frees you up to do all things you're amazing at.

You have to get the mix right, like a recipe. You have to have a great product that you can make at the right price. You have to know how to sell it with branding and marketing, so it will end up in front of the people who'll fall in love with it. You have to keep one eye on where you're at now and one eye on what you're going to do next. And never take your eye off the bank account! If you have staff, buy them cakes at least once a week. Treat them well, and they'll be there for you when the pressure's on.

One last thing, it's getting more and more important to your potential customers that there are some ethics in what you do; some integrity. For us, this includes being made in the UK. That's the question I get asked the most, after 'what's it made from? Biscuit tins!!??'

And finally...what does the future hold for Kate Hamilton Hunter Studio...any exciting plans you'd like to share?

We need to move premises as I moved here with three staff and now have eight!

I have four agents, and especially in Scotland, it's worked really well. I think the way for me to fill some gaps on my map of shops is to get more agents to certain areas of the UK. We've recently dipped our toes into the world of Facebook and Twitter and that seems to be generating more interest in what we love to do so that has some potential going forward.

As for new designs, I would like to expand into other recycled materials so I'm looking into that at the moment. I am magpie-like with the things I collect and want to include lots of new influences into my jewelry, alongside my lovely old tins!

16 SPARROWS

Name: **Kathy Zadrozny and Donovan Beeson**

Company Name: **16 Sparrows**

Founded in: **2003**

Location: **Chicago, Illinois, USA**

No. of Employees: **2 (partnership)**

Website: **www.16sparrows.com**

16 Sparrows sprouted from an observation that there were no greeting cards for sarcastic, quirky folks. Kathy Zadrozny began making her own, and after her paper goods outnumbered friends and family, she knew something had to be done! With the encouragement of two close friends, Kathy opened up shop.

In 2006 Miss Donovan joined Kathy and 16 Sparrows became a partnership. Thanks to her, 16 Sparrows has expanded its product base and has gone onto have great success at craft fairs & retail stores.

Tell us a bit about 16 Sparrows "the company". Who are you? What do you make? Where are you based?

16 Sparrows creates cards and stationery with a vintage aesthetic, but adds a sarcastic or crass twist to the item. Our cards are made for people who are not willing to sacrifice good design for humor. Donovan and I were old roommates and continue to be best friends. We are based in Chicago, our adopted home-town.

What is your background, and how did the idea to start a greetings card company come about? Did you continue to work a job while you started the company? Describe the first steps in creating your business?

I have a background in graphic design and art history while Donovan is trained in illustration. As a bright-eyed newly-graduated designer, I was unhappy at the client work I was forced to do in my "dream" advertising gig. I vented my design frustrations by creating cards and stationery for myself, as I never really saw any that fit my style or the personalities of the friends I sent these items to. I got such a good response from my designs that I thought I should take a chance at selling them online.

I created a pretty basic website using my skills from college, and html I didn't know I learned through books or online tutorials. I became a member of craft business forums and asked questions. I did research as to the best shopping cart host to use and how to price my items. Unfortunately, I did this research after I launched the website, so I had to do a lot of on-site learning and late-night price changes! The research that I made sure to do before I sold anything was test printing all of my products. I had to make sure that the printers, paper, and envelopes I had were good enough to sell. If I decided I wouldn't spend money on the final product if I were the customer, I wouldn't sell it. To this day, we never put anything for sale that we haven't tested.

How were your cards printed in those early days?

At first I printed on a bubble jet printer and paper I got from office supply stores. Since I was a designer, my first printer was pretty high quality, but I knew I could create a better looking product with a laser printer, so I saved up for that. When I earned some money I upgraded to a professional digital laser printer and started purchasing specialty paper from mills. I continued my advertising job during the day and packed orders in the evening. When I got too many orders to print and pack myself, I asked my friends to come over and help me out with the work-load in trade for food and alcohol!

In 2003, people didn't really trust "indie" businesses, so I had to put up a front as if we were a large company in order to gain people's trust that their money was safe with me. This really isn't an issue anymore, as many people seek out indie businesses now. Even so, it is still important to create an online presence that shows you are competent and trustworthy. Before I gained business credit I kept good communication with my customers, sending them a personal email about their order and the date I would ship it out. While the website was the first impression, I saw the quality of my product and my communication with the customer as the lasting one. From the beginning, I knew I wouldn't have enough money to advertise, so I had to rely on word of mouth. The happiness of my customers were, and continue to be, very important because they are our advertising. When the business grew, I didn't have time to send personal emails, so I made sure to have an automated one sent out with their orders as a confirmation. The personal touch was then transferred to the packing of their purchase: we tie up their order with ribbon, add a small thank you note, and top it with a 16 Sparrows branded pencil.

There are many designers and illustrators out there who dream of using their designs on a range of products—it's such a competitive market. What research did you do and what made you decide to take the plunge?

I took the plunge without doing research, which I would not suggest. I figured that if it failed and I got zero orders, I could just let the website expire and never do it again. Luckily, that didn't happen, so when I actually started getting orders, I realized that I needed to know what I was doing. The Switchboards (http://www.theswitchboards.com/forum/) was an amazing wealth of information and really helped me get my business cap on and learn from other people's failures and successes. I also befriended other business owners at craft fairs. As we got to know each other, we swapped info and tips. Introducing myself to these people was a little nerve wracking at first, but after you see them at three fairs in a row, it is natural that you would just say hello.

When you first started out, what were your aims? How does where you are today differ from those initial ambitions?

My initial goal was to have an arena to create designs I enjoyed and to make items for people with my sense of humor. I really felt there were no card or letter items out there for cynical or sarcastic people. I never thought I would make a living from it. Both Donovan and I continue to have day jobs, even though we do make a profit. Not having day jobs just isn't in the cards for us right now, but we do hope to drop them to do this full time eventually. I never thought I would sell cards to anyone other than my friends! Where we are today differs vastly from the start-up company of me sitting at my computer on my own designing things!

Donovan & I were originally roommates, so when we became partners we just worked together in our living room. As we moved in with our boyfriends into different apartments, we divided the work along our strengths. Donovan became the full-time maker, so she has most of the product in her living room. I tend to do the designing, web maintenance, and PR, so my office space is a little less full than hers. Beyond the splitting of apartments, we have a lot more product, so we now have a dedicated shelving areas just for our items, which we didn't have before. We also have dedicated storage and containers for craft fairs, depending on if they are indoor or outdoor. We both share our work space with our personal space, so it all comes down to insane organization to keep everything in line. We used to just make product as it was ordered, but this stopped working out for us three years into the business. We have spoken about getting a studio space, but prefer to be able to work on our product on our respective schedules and time-blocks, rather than having to force ourselves into X hours of work because we dragged ourselves through the snow to the studio.

Some items are printed by us while others we have printed on a four color press. It depends on the labor of the item, their popularity, and the look we are going for. All of our greetings cards are printed on a press because of the full color bleeds and the time that goes into folding and cutting them. They are also 16 Sparrows most popular item, so the quantity needed makes it cost-effective to get them printed on a press. Other items, like our flats, are printed on our digital printer because not too much labor goes into producing them and they are not ordered as much as our cards. If demand grows for a product and it remains steady, we price out the cost to outsource the production of that item. If we do outsource an item, we choose our printer carefully and tend to go with a company that prints with soy-based inks on recycled paper.

The amount of production for a craft fair is something we can both plan for, normally producing little by little with a few huge "making days" the week before. Any stressful large orders we get are normally from retailers. We let them know what the turnaround time is, and then just dedicate a lot of our free time to filling that order. We do try to pre-produce popular items before big shopping seasons to cope with any possible large orders, and if they don't sell, then we already have product for the fairs that season!

We are in about two dozen shops right now. We have yet to do a trade show. We don't cold call anyone and we don't have a rep. We aren't against either, we just haven't gotten around to doing it yet. We meet most of our retail connections at craft fairs. There are many retailers who shop craft fairs to see what their area is interested in, although a lot of retailers go to different cities to look for fresh product they can bring into their area. We make sure to have an inviting display and good product to back that up. Once we are stocked in a store, we maintain communication with the retailer to keep the lines open. We also respect retail boundaries—we do not sell items to any stores close to an already established retailer of ours to avoid any overlap. If a retailer has your stuff, they want to know they are THE place to get it in that area.

Are you glad you started the business? What have been the highs and lows?

I am definitely happy that I started 16 Sparrows, and there is no way I would have been able to maintain the business if it wasn't for Donovan agreeing to become my partner.

The high points have been many, starting with my first press in Daily Candy that launched 16 Sparrows out of obscurity and made me learn a lot of business lessons quick. The best high point is getting excited about new items and the enjoyable process of bringing that item to life. It is one thing that never stops being fun and we are so glad we get to do it over and over again.

The biggest low point was when I first started the business—I had absolutely no idea how much time would go into that and some of my relationships suffered. I had no idea how to separate the business from my life, which is something I've learned to do now. Whenever a product doesn't do as well as we expected, especially when we were excited about it, we also get frustrated. We try to see these as teaching points and try to learn from them the next time we create a new product, but it still stings a bit.

The only thing I would change would be to have done more research when I first started out, before I opened the business. Maybe I still would have felt flustered and crazed with all that preparation, but at least I would have had an organized base to fall back on. I also wish I would have been more willing to introduce myself to other indie business owners in the first few years of 16 Sparrows, as the ones I know now have become fast friends and a great support system. On the business aspect, we also trade info about upcoming shows and retailers with each other and are able to split costs when we travel out of town for fairs.

Where would you like the business to be in 5 years time?

Donovan & I would like to eventually quit our day jobs and open a space for ourselves. We don't necessarily mean a bricks and mortar shop, but we would love to have an open studio where people can rent typewriters, have letter writing parties, peruse our library of letter-writing books and zines. It would be more of a community space than a shop—a space where the solitary act of letter writing can turn into a shared experience.

Don't rush to open your shop. Do your research and pricing beforehand and double check before you open for business. Make sure you add *your time* into the cost of the product—your time is valuable and if you can't even pay yourself for that, who will?

Kathy Zadrozny's
Top Ten Tips for Creative Business Success

1) Start small. Don't think you need a huge variety of items to attract any and every possible customer. Have a few items that you do very well and branch out from there when you see how those do.

2) Try to do as many craft fairs/trade shows as possible. They are a lot of money up front, but you get to see and hear how customers react to your product. This is the best kind of research you can do.

3) Do not treat your competitors as your enemy. In indie businesses we all help each other out and if you do the craft fair circuit, you will be seeing these people a lot. There is no need to burn bridges just because someone is in your field of craft.

4) Always be nice to your customer, even if you think they are being rude or are wrong.

5) Do not sell anything that you wouldn't want to pay money for. Your items speak for you and you better make sure they speak well of you.

6) Use your gut. If a deal, opportunity, or wholesale purchase doesn't seem right, don't do it.

7) The presentation of a customer's order will decide how the customer will value their purchase. If you throw their items in box, you are sending the message that you don't care and that your products are not valuable. If you package the order with a personalized touch, you let your customer know that you value them and your creations.

8) Hire a good accountant. Sure, it costs money, but they can really help you out with tax breaks and deductions you would never know about and the fee is tax deductible next year.

9) You don't have to grow into a big company to be successful. Some of my favorite shops, who are running a profitable business as their only job, are one or two people operations. Do what feels right for your genre and grow as you want to grow.

10) Take time for yourself. You cannot work 24/7. Make sure to give yourself time off. These relaxing moments are when I have some of my best ideas because I step away from the work and reinvigorate my mind.

Alice ✷ PALACE

Name: **Alice Boston**

Company Name: **Alice Palace**

Founded in: **2003**

Location: **Worcestershire, UK**

Website: **www.alicepalace.co.uk**

Alice Palace is a small independent British company, specializing in unique design-led hand illustrated greetings cards.

Their beautiful studio is in Evesham in Worcestershire, standing on the banks of the Avon in the centre of the vale, Evesham is famed for fruit & vegetable market gardens.

Alice Palace is made up of a sisters act; Alice who designs all of the products and Liz the studio manager—all the work is done in house, with Alice's quirky style portrayed across each of their ranges.

'Curious illustrations and words that make you smile' is how Alice sums up her art. The more you look at the illustrations, the more you see, which is what makes them work so well. The distinctive style, charm and collage of illustration combine to make beautiful cards that can be kept as little pieces of art.

Tell us a bit about Alice Palace, the company, as it is today.

We are just in the middle of a studio move now—we'll still be in Evesham—but our new studio is a small town house which we LOVE and it even has a beautiful courtyard garden (great for the 2 dogs who come to work with us!)! It's very exciting finding new homes for everything!

I set up the company over seven years ago with the aim to create fun, eco-friendly hand-illustrated greeting cards. I quickly established a unique spot for myself on the market publishing original, positive-lifestyle cards where one design can span many occasions. My sister Lizzy joined the company two years ago as studio manager to give me more time to spend on illustrating and designing. All designs are completed in our studio and then printed as greeting cards at our uncle's factory. We mostly sell to independent gift shops.

What is your career/design background? How did the idea for the business come about?

I have always loved art and, following art GCSE and A Level I chose to pick a subject I really enjoyed at university and went for a graphic design course at Nottingham Trent where I got a first. The idea for Alice Palace first came about when I was showing the owner of a gallery my illustrations and she said they'd work really well as greeting cards. Firstly I picked 8 of my favorite drawings and then started research into shops in my local area, asking them if they would stock my designs. When a handful of shops said yes, I did my first print run and following that, my first trade show at Top Drawer in London (which was very scary!). I wouldn't have said that I had a plan, or any aims other than trying to get shops to order and then sell my cards. I was working part time in a design studio alongside setting up my own company, until the time came for the big leap into full time Alice Palace!

I think I went into it a bit blind to be honest! I guess I've always had an eye on the greeting card world without really realizing it, and I love writing and sending cards myself. I wouldn't say I really 'took the plunge' until I went full time and that happened when I was made redundant from my part time job—a blessing in disguise and the best thing I ever did—now I cannot believe I didn't do it sooner!!

Please describe the space you work from? Has this changed from when you started out?

As I said before, we're just in the middle of a studio move now—we were after a few things: more space, a ground floor place with our own front door, no leaks in the roof and warmth in the winter! Our new studio is a small but perfect town house which we LOVE! Downstairs it has a work room, a room for eating/having meetings, a tiny kitchen and loo and then a lovely walled courtyard garden that reminds me of the secret garden! Upstairs there are three rooms; a crafty room, a storage room for all our trade show stuff and a tiny room for Albert (who's my 9 month old son). We're all very excited about it!

The studio we're moving from is above a pet shop which my Mum used to own. We've been there for two years and moved in when Lizzy joined the company because there wasn't enough room for her to join me when I was working from home! I didn't realize how great it would be to have a studio rather than work from home, until it actually happened! When working from home it is very difficult to switch off. I'd think 'I'll just do this' and before I knew it hours would have passed! Having a studio means you can get away from work, which I think is a very good thing—although at the beginning, you do have to (and want to) put all your living hours into it—so it is good to be working from home at the start for that reason, as well as the obvious money reasons.

For anyone thinking of getting their own studio, my advice would be looking at it in the day so you can see how much light there is. Check for damp as well. Heating's a nice thing—we didn't have any for two years so wore lots of clothes and hats and gloves and scarves. We got all furniture second hand to save money.

Trade Fairs—An expensive, but necessary tool? Discuss.

I think that trade shows are really good—the reasons being:

They get you OUT THERE, in the real world, facing customers. Your work is pitched against competitors, which makes you work hard.

For me they serve as being a kind of boss—they make me do new work and make me have deadlines. I think otherwise, when you work for yourself, it's very easy to just drift along.

Before I did my first trade show I went to look round 2 of the big UK trade shows —Top Drawer in London and the Spring Fair in Birmingham, and chose to do Top Drawer because I found it a much more enjoyable experience wandering round the design-led exhibitor stands there. We still do Top Drawer Spring and Top Drawer Autumn every year, and they are still really good shows for us. I did Spring Fair for three years running and think it's something that's good to do, but isn't necessarily that fun to do; too long, too big. We've also tried out different summer shows like Pulse, PGL and the Summer Fair, and tend to do three or four trade shows a year.

The first show I did was very scary as I didn't even know what pro-forma meant, and had to ask the customer to explain it to me! Now I really enjoy the shows—it's nice meeting up with other publishers who have become friends, and it's fun to be in London for a few days and get the 'London Look'!! It's great meeting up with our customers and getting face to face feedback on existing designs and our new designs launched at the shows. Lows would include achy feet, extreme tiredness, and really hot hotel rooms!

With greetings card being a fairly low value item, you must need to sell lots to make any profit. Do you have minimum orders for retailers in order to make all the admin of an order worthwhile?

We don't just sell greeting cards, we sell lots of other products too. We do have minimum orders for trade—ours is £85. We thought this was a reasonable amount —you have to do what you feel comfortable with.

With 7 years in business so far—what have been the high points? And lows? With the benefit of hindsight, is there anything you'd do differently?

We've now been in business seven whole years and I cannot believe it!!! High points are;

I LOVE designing and really enjoy it when I can get completely lost in it and suddenly have lots of new design ideas.

Being your own boss has its rewards and working when it suits you is great.

I think seeing all your designs up at a trade show is very exciting as it's the only time that you get to see the illustrations all at once.

The worst time was probably when our studio roof sprung a leak and I was constantly worrying every time it rained about everything getting ruined.

In addition to all the cards and other items you design and sell, you also take on commissions and do wedding invitations. How do such commissions come about—word of mouth or do you advertise?

Commissions come about from the sale of greeting cards—as our website and products/services offered are listed on the back of our cards. We haven't had to do any advertising which is great—although we do plan to do a wedding show sometime in the future. The wedding section of our business is different from the greeting card part because we are much more involved with the customer. Doing both works well, but involves lots of time planning and a great studio manager!!

Production—do you print in-house or outsource to a printing company?

We do both. We print in house (and did lots of research into getting the right machinery for the card that we wanted to print on), and we also use local printers when we have very large orders (we use Severnprint in Gloucester because they are a very green company and do a great job).

You are a member of several industry trade bodies—which ones, and why? What are the benefits to your business?

We are a member of DACS—The Design and Artists Copyright Society. They provide legal advice to artists and also work to ensure that artists' rights are respected and that these rights are recognized both financially and morally. Their payback scheme is worth applying for—this year DACS has £4 million of Payback royalties to distribute amongst visual artists whose work has been reproduced in UK books and magazines or on certain UK television channels. Any type of visual artist can make a claim—fine artists, illustrators, photographers, graphic designers, architects, sculptors, craft makers and cartoonists have all made successful claims in past years.

FSB—The Federation of Small Businesses is the UK's largest campaigning pressure group promoting and protecting the interests of the self-employed and owners of small firms. They offer support for all topics of business.

GCA—The Greeting Card Association. The GCA is an independent not for profit organization owned by its members. It provides wide-ranging industry information and specialist resources for publishers, artists and writers; help, advice, support and wide-ranging membership services.

NOTHS—Not on the High Street—We joined NOTHS when they first started, and we support all their work. It's a business set up by friends Holly and Sophie to source unique products that aren't found in shops on the High Street. Their marketing department is first class and we find them very supportive of our products.

AOI—The Association of Illustrators. The AOI actively campaigns to maintain and protect the rights of their members. They give advice on the following areas: Portfolio advice, publications, client directories, business advice, discounts, legal advice, advice to students and new illustrators, and online portfolios.

You also sell on Not On The High Street—kind of like a slicker, UK version of Etsy—how long have you sold through them? Do you make good sales? Is it worth other designers trying, particularly as you now have to pay to join?

We have been with NOTHS since the very beginning. It's is very worthwhile for us and like everything, the more you put in, the more you get out (I struggled to find the time for it before Lizzy joined me). I think it's worth it not just for the sales, but for the advertising—you get potentially seen by such a large audience, which will not happen from your own website for a good long while.

Words of wisdom! What sort of advice do you wish you had been given before you started out?

If you're setting up as a greeting card publisher: source your envelope before deciding on a card size! Otherwise you end up with a bespoke size like me (which costs more!!).

At first Alice Palace was just fun and more like a hobby to me, and it is still fun, but you do have to remember that it is a business! I really struggle with accounts. It's best to concentrate on what you are good at, and pay others to do the things you're not so good at.

Go with your instinct, it's good to take on advice from others, but you have to do what you feel is right. That's what makes your business stand out!

And finally…what does the future hold for Alice Palace…any exciting plans you'd like to share?

We'd really like to do a wedding show, but at the moment we're very excited about our new studio and making it all Alice Palace-ey!

crow *and* canary
fine art card + gift representation

Name: **Carina Murray**

Company Name: **Crow and Canary**

Founded in: **2006**

Location: **Portland, Oregon, USA**

No. of Reps: **4**

Website: **www.crowandcanary.com**

Crow and Canary is a travel-based repping agency, specializing in Fine Art, Card & Gift Representation, covering territories including Oregon, Washington, California, New York, New Jersey and Connecticut. A focus on handmade products, eco-friendly practices and a talented line up of local and national designers, are just a few of the qualities that set Crow and Canary apart in the industry

Founded by Carina Murray in 2006, the company has gone on to represent a diverse line up of designers – though letterpress, screen-printed and hand embellished cards remain at the core of the collection. Carina is a true champion of independent stationers and hopes that her passion and adoration for her job comes through via her blog and many social media endeavors. You can most often find Carina with her trusty canine companion, Ula, en route to show eager shops the latest and greatest from the C&C collection!

You represent a great selection of greetings card and stationery companies—so, what exactly does a "Rep" do then?

Reps are essentially a liaison between the designer and wholesale buyer. We show samples to buyers and forward the orders on to the lines we represent. We are not responsible for production or shipping. Our job is strictly commission-based, 10-25% is the industry norm. Most reps only take commission on orders paid, meaning if a retailer cancels the order or does not follow through with payment, the rep doesn't receive commission.

I work primarily as a traveling rep. I visit stores in the Pacific NW and have three additional sub-reps that call on their own territories. We work much in the fashion of an old-school traveling salesman. We also exhibit at several trade shows a year, including the *New York International Gift Fair* and the *National Stationery Show*. Participation in trade shows is optional and requires a participation fee, along with standard commission. This is an excellent option for most designers, as exhibiting at a trade show as a single entity is a rather large undertaking and expense.

Tell us a bit about your background—what were you doing before founding Crow and Canary, and when/where did the idea for the business come from?

My degree is in fine art photography; I interned at a photography gallery in Seattle, Washington during college and went on to work as the assistant director after graduating. I also have a background in the optical world, having worked on and off as an Optician for many years, that was my fallback trade before I launched my company. Having primarily worked for small business owners, I have had some excellent mentors to learn from and many of the bits of wisdom that I've picked up translate to any industry.

In 2006 I'd become a bit burned out at my 9-5 job. I had recently met a designer with a successful card company and began helping her with production and fulfillment on the side. She planted the seed that working as a manufacturer's representative could be a low overhead and flexible business idea and she happened to be looking for a rep on the West Coast. I was quite excited about the thought, as I've always been a stationery fanatic and during college spent some time printmaking and setting type for letterpress. I quit my day job in September of 2006 and Crow and Canary was officially born!

Describe the early days of your business? How did you make ends meet? Do you remember your first sale/order? How long did it take before you were making enough to live on?

Business was slow going at first. I started representing just one line; I now work with 28 manufacturers. I was fortunate that both retailers and designers were willing to take a chance on me.

I distinctly remember the initial nervousness of cold-calling stores and stopping in to introduce myself. My first order was with a well-known Los Angeles paper boutique and they continue to be a loyal account. I'm forever grateful that they were welcoming to me and helped build my confidence to keep reaching out to retailers. I would estimate that it took over 12 months before I was able to support myself through the business. I was fortunate to have a savings account to dip into and my husband was able to provide us health insurance benefits through his employer.

What do you look for when taking on a new brand?

I'm rather specific in what I look for when I consider adding a new line to my repertoire. Here are a few of my considerations:

- The line must be complementary to my current collection; if it's too similar to designs I already represent, I risk competition within my own collection.
- I'm always on the lookout for innovative products. If I see a line and think: "Wow, that's so unique"—it's definitely a contender.
- Good product photography, a comprehensive website and catalog and flexibility are key.
- I find it easier to rep lines that have at least 40 unique designs, though this is not a hard and fast rule.
- Lines that work with eco-friendly goods are also a plus.

Would you ever Rep a designer/brand who had literally just designed their first range and hadn't yet sold into stores themselves? Or do you prefer them to have established a track record in their area first?

I believe it's vital that designers do as much for their brand themselves as they can initially. There is a refinement process that happens for most new lines and it's invaluable to receive direct feedback about pricing, designs, paper quality, etc. I typically tell designers to "wear as many hats" within their company as they can, for as long as they can. There will come a point when tasks, including sales, need to be delegated and that is usually when working with a rep is the next natural step.

I rarely approach brand new manufacturers. I do think a good track record is important and I take a lot of feedback under consideration from the shop owners and buyers that I work with. If I consistently hear that a line is selling well and that the designer is easy to work with, I'm more likely to approach that line if it fits my aesthetic.

At what stage in the business did you take on your first employee—was it a big leap from doing everything yourself to hiring others? How did you know you were ready and the business could afford it?

I had toyed with the idea of hiring a sub-rep for several years, but never seriously pursued it. I'd gone as far as including a blurb on my website that said I was seeking a sub-rep in the San Francisco/Bay Area. I'd occasionally receive an inquiry from someone, mostly folks without any background in the stationery industry. In April of 2010, Kendra Gjerseth contacted me—she couldn't have been a better match! Kendra had been a paper boutique owner and manufacturer in the stationery world and was looking to start a career in the repping world. It was really an easy and natural transition, I didn't have much to lose as I was simply paying her for orders that she generated and providing her with some sales materials and tools. Having Kendra onboard really changed the way I viewed my business, I've since gone on to hire two additional reps in other territories and I am open to the idea of expanding into more areas if I were to find the right people.

The greetings card market is so competitive these days? Any advice for new young designers about to take the leap?

Definitely attend the *National Stationery Show* and/or a major wholesale gift show near you and see what you're up against. It's really important to walk the show floor and see what other people are selling. Perhaps your million-dollar idea was just launched by another company. Know who your competitors are and figure out the edge that you offer that sets your brand apart.

Take part in social networking; I was a naysayer myself—I won't lie. Twitter alone has completely revolutionized my business. I've been able to develop relationships with buyers, designers and press that would not have otherwise been accessible to me. Be a part of industry conversations. Establish yourself as a knowledgeable go-to person. Positive, tangible benefits will follow, I promise!

I love creative and unique greetings, but don't forget to focus on occasions that sell. You can never have too many birthday cards, with thank you and love coming in as a close second. Listen to what buyers need; if you're working with a store that says they can't find enough good sympathy cards create a design to fill that need if it fits within your brand.

How should new designers go about finding the right Rep for them?

An online presence of independent sales reps and repping agencies is surprisingly low. These are some of the routes I know of:

- *The National Stationery Show* typically has a listing in the lobby of the convention center for 'Rep's seeking Lines' and vice-versa. If you are exhibiting at a wholesale show, place a "reps wanted" sign in your booth.

- Most gift show and wholesale tradeshow websites list the names of reps exhibiting in current or past shows. You may consider checking out a local wholesale gift show to introduce yourself to some reps. It's usually not too hard to gain a free day pass if you're able to show your business credentials to the show manager.

- Ask some of the retailers you work with. I frequently get inquiries from designers that have gotten my name from buyers I do business with.

- Ask other designers you're friendly with, not everyone is willing to share this sort of information, but it never hurts to ask.

- Lastly, get creative with your google searches. 'Manufacturer's Representative' is only a jumping off point in terms of keywords.

Once you sign up with a rep for a certain region, do you have to pay them commission for any and all shops you have product in within that region? What if you already had shops in place before you signed on with them? What if shops approach you directly without having ever interacted with the rep?

This will definitely vary by rep. I personally write individual contracts for new lines and am usually willing to negotiate, regarding existing accounts. One thing to consider—designers typically receive re-orders more steadily when working with reps, as reps tend to see stores on a quarterly basis. Although you'd be out the commission, you'd likely be ahead in the long run. There are some stores that prefer to order directly from the designer. Because these are few and far between, most of the lines I work with still pay commission on these orders. If you are considering working with a rep, I'd recommend that you get answers to these questions directly and be sure to draw up a contract that restates all of the information you and the rep agreed to verbally.

Any tips for approaching buyers and getting my line into stores myself?

I would encourage any line looking for more exposure to send press kits to magazines, as well as emails to design blogs. In terms of contacting out-of-town stores, my method is to first call and politely request the name of the buyer. I typically mention that it's for the purpose of sending catalogs and rarely have anyone decline to give me the contact name. From there, I would go all out in creating a package for your catalog that's enticing to open. You may consider using themes from your line. Brand cohesiveness and a bit of ingenuity go a long way! Your mailing will be memorable and stand out among the many submissions stores receive. Be sure to follow-up by phone or email. Tenacity is key! In a perfect world, you wouldn't have to follow-up with stores, they'd see the product and order it that instant. However, I find that most buyers have so much going on that they don't mind a few reminder emails or calls. Unless a buyer explicitly says they aren't interested, I continue to stay in contact with them.

Because greetings cards are relatively low value items, what sort of wholesale minimums would you suggest?

$100 is the average minimum order and I find that most stores don't have a problem reaching minimums. It's perfectly appropriate to have a minimum on paper, but be willing to be flexible with stores if they request a reduced minimum. If your cards sell well they will surely order above the minimum next time. It's really about building lasting relationships with retailers, so be willing to break your own rules sometimes. Most cards are sold in 6's and occasionally dozens. Most of the stores I work with prefer to buy in 6's, as that allows them a larger selection of designs. Gift items and items with higher price points are often sold in 3's or 4's.

Because of the fairly low price points/profit margins of greetings cards, you would need to sell pretty high volume every month to earn a decent living. I guess those sort of production numbers are achievable when using a commercial printer, but is it hard for designers to produce, and earn a living from, hand-made /hand-printed cards?

The advantage of printing your own goods is that you don't have to stock a large inventory, which can be challenging to find space for and it's often hard to predict which styles will sell well. The initial investment is also lower, since you can print to order if necessary, whereas commercial printers require high minimums per piece in order to get a price break. It's also easy to prototype designs and wait for feedback. If a style is not well received it can be scrapped without much loss.

The disadvantage of printing your own goods is that the production time can be a bit long and tedious and if it becomes necessary to hire production help, this can also begin to gobble up profit margins. I have seen a handful of companies that have gone under from not being able to keep up with the success and production demands as they grow. I think a good business plan and a reliable team can help circumvent that sort of demise.

It's imperative to time your seasonal releases with the industry standards. This really is a case of "the early bird gets the worm"! Buyers begin writing holiday orders (Halloween, Christmas, Hanukkah) as early as May and June. It's really easy to miss out on a large chunk of sales if your new designs aren't ready to show. Another big seasonal release is Valentine's Day. I start showing Valentine's as early as October. Most buyers don't see reps between Thanksgiving and Christmas, so it's definitely helpful to have these out early. For spring occasions (Easter, Mother's Day, Father's Day and Graduation) I would recommend a release date in early January.

Having just brought on a full-time rep in Los Angeles and the New York tri-state area 7 months ago, I'm really focusing my energy on helping grow those territories. For the first time, Crow & Canary will have booths at the winter and summer *New York International Gift Fair* and *The National Stationery Show* this year. This is a big and exciting undertaking for us and we know will lead to some new opportunities. I've also been expanding my consulting offerings for manufacturers that are new to the industry.

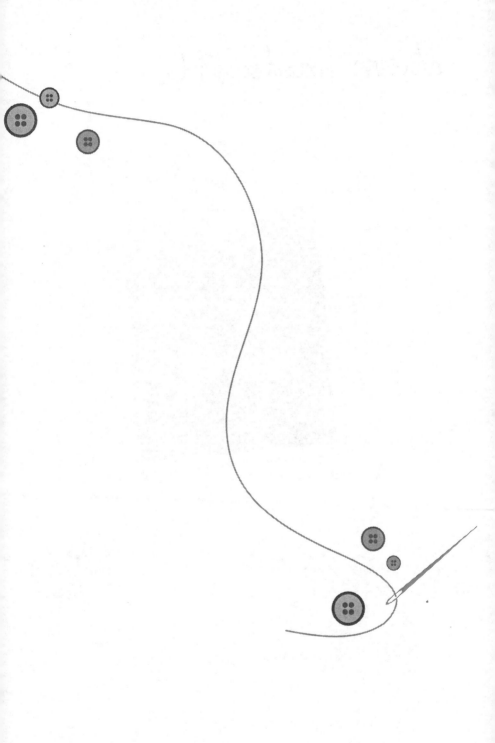

alison hardcastle

Name: **Alison Hardcastle**

Company Name: **Alison Hardcastle**

Founded in: **2005**

Location: **Yorkshire, UK**

Website: **www.alisonhardcastle.co.uk**

Alison Hardcastle is an illustrator, designer, printmaker and book artist living and working in Yorkshire, UK.

After studying Illustration at Edinburgh College of Art followed by an MA at Brighton University, Alison returned to Yorkshire and set up her studio at home and print studio nearby. Alison Hardcastle cards, books, stationery and prints was founded in 2005 and born out of a love of illustration, beautiful books and stationery, handmade things, screen printing, colors, patterns, words, type, phrases, languages, structures and buildings, cities, the countryside, car boot sales and second hand shops, collections and finding ways of organizing, recording and documenting all of these. (Oh and not forgetting tea and cake!!)

The collection now comprises an extensive range of high quality hand screen printed cards, books, stationery and prints displaying bold patterns, hand drawn lettering and illustrative elements distributed to shops both big and small throughout the UK. Integral to all Alison's work is her passion for the handmade and hand printed. Everything is designed, printed and made by Alison herself in-house. Alison is constantly scribbling down phrases, drawing out ideas, taking photographs and designing new products to extend and refresh the range. Alongside her range of products Alison has applied her illustrative skills to a number of commissions, bespoke stationery, editorial and design work.

You launched your business in 2005 at your home in Yorkshire. Describe the first steps in creating your business?

In 2005 I left a full time job as a visual merchandiser at the furniture and home-wares retailer Habitat to launch my own business as a self-employed illustrator and designer. I had been doing bits and pieces of creative work in my spare time while working at Habitat (mainly artists' books and a bit of teaching) but was incredibly frustrated at not having the time to do much illustration and work at what I loved doing—being creative.

I left and found a part-time job at a lovely independent design shop in York called Snowhome and worked a couple of days a week alongside expanding my artist book work and beginning a small range of cards. I sold these at artists book fairs and started to get a few small orders from independent shops and galleries. I also continued to teach as a visiting lecturer/tutor in bookbinding and illustration at Edinburgh College of Art a few days a term.

I didn't really have a plan—everything just evolved along the way. My cards started selling well and I had more and more interest and orders from shops and galleries and it started to grow from there. Working in a small shop helped enormously as I also gained a valuable insight into the 'other side of the fence'—seeing what a buyer/retailer looks for as well as getting a lot of business help, support and experience from Angus who owns Snowhome.

It is a partnership which has lasted beyond me working at the shop and we now collaborate creatively where possible—I recently completed a print commission for a typographic word map of the British Isles for Snowhome.

There are tons of graphic designers and illustrators out there who dream of using their designs on a range of products—it's such a competitive market. What research did you do and what made you decide to take the plunge?

I guess I didn't really think of it as embarking on trying to get my designs out there and on products. I love designing and screen printing and was just happy to be making things and doing my own work. The cards were always incidental to my artists books and illustration work in my mind—so when this part of my business really started to take off it wasn't really a planned strategy! The fact that the greetings card market is such a competitive one didn't really occur to me as it happened so gradually. There was never a 'grand plan'—as a typical creative person I was just doing what I loved and was ecstatic if someone wanted to spend their money on it and like it too! I'd love to say I embarked on it all with a plan but I'm afraid I didn't even do any research as such—apart from being an avid design/creative/ interiors magazine reader and loving looking at beautiful card and stationery.

You produce a range of paper products, all hand printed by you. Do you do all the work yourself or employ any help? How have you managed to upscale production as your business has grown. How do you cope when a massive order comes in, and busy times such as after a big trade show?

This is something which is troubling me greatly at the moment. I love to print everything myself as it's 'hands on' and I can control the colors, size of print run and experiment a lot more. Plus I still get to be a printmaker. However as I get busier—especially in the last 6-9 months—I'm finding it harder to keep up, and end up spending all my time printing, folding and packing cards and packing orders. I don't yet employ anyone, mainly as it seems like a big step to me and I don't have a very big studio at home—only room for me at present! As much as I would love to carry on printing everything myself, especially as I've always marketed my products as hand-printed, I'm going to have to outsource this soon to free up my time for designing and expanding my range as well as doing more commissions.

Please describe the space you work from?

I started in the spare room of our old house and I've now progressed to the garage of our current house. It's a room in the garage that has at some time conveniently been turned into an office/work space. It's a cosy little space and I love working from home and all the comforts that entails. I can nip back in the house for a coffee when I want and take a break sitting in my garden on a sunny day! I can hide myself away in the peace and quiet (no 2 year olds allowed in there!) without distraction.

I print in my own print studio which I was lucky enough to set up at my parents farm close by. It's a lovely big space and I have a built-in babysitter (my mum!) so it works all round. I set it up very gradually over the space of a couple of years— patiently buying bits of screen printing equipment from ebay when I could afford them.

What was the first Trade Fair you showed at? Which shows do you still do?

My trade fair experiences have on the whole been very positive. I've only ever done the same fair—Pulse at Earls Court in London, but I think it's a great show. I've always been in the Launchpad section of the show which is for small designers and companies like myself and it's a great atmosphere between exhibitors. I've grown in confidence and experience over the 3 years I've done it and now know what needs to be done before the show, the best way to build-up and take down and little things to make it smoother, easier and slightly less stressful.

Selling to retailers—for the benefit of those not yet wholesaling, how do you calculate your wholesale price to retailers?

This was a tricky area when I first started. I based my wholesale price on others in the market doing a similar thing and also what I felt people would pay for a hand screen printed card. I did do costings for my cards and worked out my margins but a hand screen printed card is always going to have a lot more time involved in it than a commercially printed one, so I had to reflect this in the trade price. The larger retailers have a bigger mark-up than the smaller shops so consequently want things as cheap as possible—there's always quite an exchange of emails/phone calls when trying to come to an agreed price with a big retailer! On the flip-side though they're in a position to place large orders and regular repeat orders so this has to be taken into account too.

With greetings card being a fairly low value item, you must need to sell lots to make any profit. Do you have minimum orders for retailers in order to make all the admin of an order worthwhile?

I don't have a minimum order and never have as I was anxious to appeal to the smaller independent shops and they sometimes like to 'test the water' a little first and just stock a few of my range to see how it goes. I do carriage paid over £100 as an incentive for them to order more. My advice to new designers would be not to have a large minimum order. In the current climate smaller retailers in particular want to check that something will sell before they stock a large quantity and it's best to get them as a stockist first and then they'll hopefully come back for repeat orders. It's important to get them on board rather than putting them off with a huge minimum order.

6 years in business so far—what have been the high points? And lows? With the benefit of hindsight, is there anything you'd do differently?

High points have been my trade shows—the first one in particular as I realized that I had products that appealed to many people and shops wanted to stock them.

This year has been a significant point as my business has reached a new level and I'm busier than ever. I now need to match this by looking at what I need to do to allow the business to grow and how I can outsource things like printing and packing to make the best use of my time. This will then leave me free to do more designing and I can expand the ranges of products.

I can't think of any specific low points. Sometimes when I'm working every evening until late I wonder when I'll ever get the work/life balance right (but doesn't everyone?) but that's the nature of having your own business. I find it hard to switch off and on the rare occasion that I haven't got a long list of work to do I find something to do in my studio on an evening anyway!

With hindsight I wouldn't change anything much as it's all got me to the point I'm at today. I built things up very gradually compared to some businesses, but this wasn't through a lack of determination, but more a need to work and earn money which made me a little more cautious.

You also have a small daughter—how do you run a business, juggle family life, and stay sane?

I'm not the best person to ask as my business does take over sometimes! I'm very fortunate to have a very supportive family and husband but I do struggle to juggle everything. Martha goes to nursery and her grandparents throughout the week with at least a couple of half days with me. It's very difficult—especially making myself work on a evening if I have an order to pack once bath time and bed time are finished. My mum looks after her while I print as my print studio is at their farm and so I get to see her throughout the day and she visits me in my print room to watch me print. Hopefully soon she'll be able to help!

Words of wisdom! What sort of advice do you wish you had been given before you started out?

I'm often contacted by students wanting advice or tips for setting up. I always tell them to be patient and not to expect everything to happen overnight as sometimes, as in my case, it all builds up over time. I've found that gaining as much business experience as possible is essential. Working in Snowhome taught me a lot about keeping books, invoicing, dealing with buyers and conducting yourself in a business-like way.

And finally…what does the future hold for Alison Hardcastle…any exciting plans you'd like to share?

I'd love to keep developing my range of cards further and also begin litho or digitally printing my cards and stationery. Plus I keep getting asked about applying my designs to other surfaces such as fabric and mugs so watch this space!

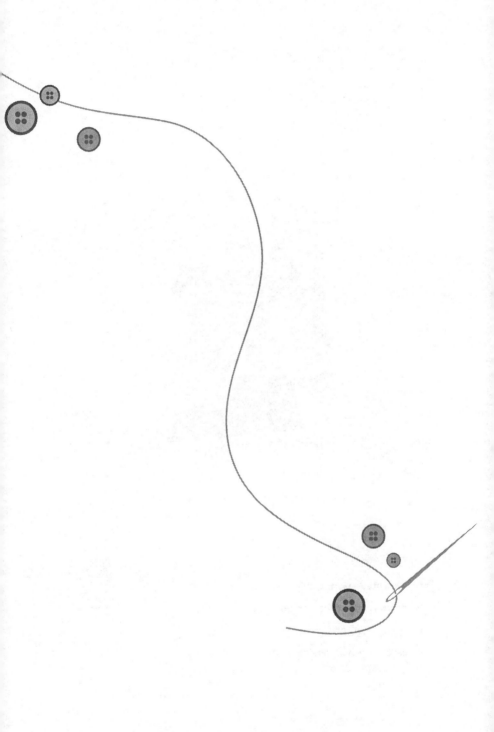

Name: **Nora Alexander and Maie Iiis Webb**

Company Name: **Noon Design**

Location: **California, USA**

Website: **www.noondesignshop.com**

Noon Designs is a collection of hand-fabricated jewelry and paper goods. The designers Nora Alexander + Maie Liis Webb have joined together to create a unique design studio and two storefronts in the heart of Ocean Beach in San Diego and Solana Beach, California.

Nora Alexander: Jewelry Designer. Nora is originally from Rhode Island and was trained as an industrial designer at the Rhode Island School of Design. After several years in the jewelry industry she launched her own line, focusing on creating individual pieces whose inspiration is drawn from the natural world. Maie Liis Webb: Graphic Designer. Originally from the Jersey Shore, Maie graduated from RISD with a BFA in Graphic Design. She moved to San Diego in 2003 with a passion for creating paper goods, specifically letterpress wedding and special occasion invitations. Her attention to detail and drive to create handmade objects led her to the thriving wedding scene in San Diego.

Tell us about Noon Design, the company as it stands today?

Noon designs is based in San Diego, California, and we are primarily made up of jewelry and paper goods, with two storefronts here in SD, and we wholesale around the country and internationally in approx 70 stores. We create custom work through our shops, specifically in the bridal industry, focusing on wedding invitations and custom bridal jewelry. Noon has branched out in the past year into more of a lifestyle brand creating other Noon products such as our perfume "noonscents", glassware, and textiles. We feel there are endless possibilities for our designs and we are slowly testing the waters of other alleys we can go down.

What did you each do before you launched the company? Were you already working separately before starting Noon together?

We originally met in college at the Rhode Island School of Design where we were roommates, and spent a few stints abroad together studying photography and graphic design in Slovakia and Switzerland. We knew we worked and traveled well together, so after college we moved to Southern California and worked in the restaurant industry to get by, and for a few years flip-flopped between the east and west coast. Nora worked for both silversmiths and goldsmiths in California and New York City, her passion shifting from large scale furniture/ industrial design to a more feasible and accessible craft of jewelry design. I continued to work in the hospitality industry for several years, but had a steady flow of graphic design projects, assuring myself of my ultimate goal of owning my own business. By the end of 2008 we both landed on the west coast again, and it was then we decided it was time to finally team up and start something. We had talked about many ideas in the past—brick pizza shop, retail storefront—we didn't care, we just wanted something to call our own and to work for ourselves!

By the time we teamed up Nora had already been working full-time as a jewelry designer under her own name. She had her jewelry line in probably 10 shops at this time, mainly on consignment. I was still working as a bartender and by this time was seriously looking for a way out! We decided to join forces and go with what we knew, and not reinvent the wheel.

Nora was already designing jewelry and I was creating paper goods, hence Noon was born. We figured that with a graphic designer on board we could start to establish a look and feel for the Noon brand. With two heads and hands we could accomplish so much more, attend more shows, produce more products and grow our wholesale accounts. It makes all aspects of the business that much easier when you have another voice that you trust to bounce ideas off of. We were a great duo, the jewelry designs were simple and nice on their own but with the packaging design and the company branding, it really made the company complete.

We worked out of Nora's house for the first few months and eventually moved into a very small affordable retail/office space down the street. Originally we were thinking of the space just as a studio work space, but since it had street access we decided to open it up to the public as a working studio with a small retail section— we thought it would be neat to share the creative process with the consumer. This concept was very well received by our customers, they enjoyed meeting us and it really helped to create a story about the products and the company.

We both worked seven days a week and basically didn't let any opportunity pass by. We were at every show, even little local elementary school meet and greet events to generate a following. It was baby steps to establish a true and faithful customer base. We truly value each and every customer, and we rely heavily, still to this day, on word of mouth.

We thought it was important to draw you picture of what kind of space we were working with in our first shop—we're talking a total of 240 square foot work/retail space—it was basically a renovated garage. It was located in a small San Diego neighborhood known as Ocean Beach. The Noon Shop was a block away from the main strip of the community, but we were tucked away surrounded mostly by residential buildings, not a retailer's dream location! But we eventually saved up some money got a cute turquoise awning with our handmade wooden Noon sign mounted on it, which definitely helped to draw the people in. Once inside we divided the space in half, one side retail, the other our work space, so it was a very cozy little space!

During the early days we would hand make EVERYTHING—we didn't have the money to buy other products like we do today to fill the space (I know it sounds silly that we would have a hard time filling such a tiny space but remember jewelry and greeting cards are quite small things). There was no back-stock, so when we sold something we had to make another one and that sometimes meant waiting a few days till the material arrived to make it. So we would literally use the leftover paper scraps from wedding invites and make gift tags, journals or coasters. There were many "one of a kind" items back then!

When you first started out, what were your aims?

We were ready to make a name for ourselves in the industry! We didn't get ahead of ourselves and we knew it wouldn't happen overnight by any means, and that there was going to have to be a lot of longs hours, traveling, and connecting with people to make it happen. We still have that goal and it is always a work in progress to better our business.

Taking on a retail premises is a huge step for any designer/maker. How did you know you were ready?

We had an advantage of using the space for both our studio space and as a storefront. We knew we would have to pay rent for a studio, so why not open the doors, and any money that comes in from selling our goods was a bonus. We wanted the wholesale jewelry business and the custom graphic design projects to make the money and not depend on foot traffic, and shop sales to keep us a float. We lucked out with inexpensive rent and I think the charm of such a teeny tiny space worked in our favor. We had no running water or bathroom, it was bare bones that we made pretty and welcoming. The retail space worked for us, and since we made all of our products we didn't have to put up tons of money for inventory. Our products were produced with time and a smaller amount of money for materials, and we also both really enjoyed creating spaces that were inviting and creative. It worked out well that our products fit into our space.

Opening a retail space also worked out so well for us because fortunately Maie is amazing at visual merchandising. Some people enjoy just making things and having someone else sell it, but we truly enjoyed both. We feel that the connection between the user and maker is really important and has had a great effect on our new business. We opened in early 2009 when the US economy really hit rock bottom. People were watching the money but the life went on, there were still birthdays and anniversaries that people had to buy for and they started paying attention to where their money was going.

For any of those who are thinking of opening a retail space of your own, ask yourself a few questions: Are you a people person? Do you really love what you do and are willing to do it every day? Most stores are open on weekends/holidays, are you willing to work on them?.

Nora still makes all of the jewelry, and we employ a couple of gals that help out with the production. We looked into getting our ear-wires massed produced overseas and just couldn't do it! It goes against what we stand for and we'd much rather figure out a way to make everything in-house or in the USA. Maie recently had a baby so was forced to streamline the greeting card line and have them printed locally. This was such a blessing because now we are getting them letterpress printed in San Diego, and she is still able to be a part of the process by being there the entire time while they are printed to oversee everything. In turn Maie has started to learn how to make the ear-wires, which are a huge part of the jewelry productions. Nora still works 6 days a week making the jewels to keep up with the demand!

You now wholesale your goods to other stores—how has that developed?

We are currently in over 70 stores at this time, solely from doing trade shows ourselves and without using reps. We did our first "trade" show in the winter of 2009—the Boston Gift Show. It was such a great learning experience! We were able to talk with other vendors and get advice, and learn some terms like "Net 30"! We were total rookies, but it was okay. Retailers loved the fact that we were the product, and that we made each piece and it was so "homegrown". Not to mention they loved our price point—we didn't quite know how to price things for wholesale and maybe lost some money at first, but slowly found that balance with keeping our prices accessible without losing our shirts!

As both designer/makers AND retailers, you get to see things from both sides of the fence. For those wishing to wholesale their handmade items into stores, what tips would you give them for approaching retailers?

We now sell other locally-made items and products from other independent designers from around the country in our shops. We keep it simple and don't overwhelm our customers with tons of different products, just well- made and quality items. We did need to bring in other items just because it is incredibly hard to make all of your products by hand in your shop. When something sells it's wonderful, but you can't simply put in an order for more, you have to take the time and make it again. The other products help fill in and compliment the jewelry and paper goods. Like I mentioned earlier, we started having other "noon" products made locally or in the USA. We design them and have them made and are involved in the entire process. Being those gals on the other side of the fence, we know how hard and intimidating it is to try and sell your products to other retail shops. We have a couple of tips we picked up along the years. Even if you are good at selling things, it can be really difficult to sell your own products. It might help if you have a friend who knows and enjoys your product that can "represent" your line and talk to retailers. Also, do your research—check out what products stores carry and make sure yours would be a good fit. You don't want to waste time talking to a shop that is not the right fit for you. Lastly, we would say try calling or emailing first. This doesn't always have to happen but in our case it's hard if an artist comes into the shop wanting to show us their goods and we are busy helping customers. So make an appointment with the owner or retail buyer or at least ask if this is a good time, so that you and your product can get the attention you deserve.

Cashflow—the main problem with most small businesses! How did you finance the growth of your business?

It is always scary to make sure you have enough money to pay your employees, rent, utilities, sale tax and of course yourselves! Even if business is growing rapidly, so do the bills! We started with contributing just over $2000 each, that's it! We didn't go to banks or any outside sources. We started very small, making everything ourselves, only purchasing materials when we needed them. We didn't go out and buy computers or fancy display items, we worked with what we had, used our existing tools and scavenged our homes and garage sales for items to set up the shop. I think the best things happen when you have limited funds, as it forces you to be resourceful and get extra creative! Nora and I moved in baby steps to get the shop going, getting an awning after six months, maybe a year to get a good computer. We just did little moves at a time to get by!

What has been the absolute stand-out best moment of your business career so far? And the worst?

I don't know if for me there is just one stand out moment, it is all of the little things! I love having our customers tell us stories about seeing our jewels across the country on strangers, or getting a great new account, or the excitement of getting into the handmade section of the New York Gift Fair. The worst was dealing with the building that our original space was in when it went into foreclosure, and the uncertainty of the future of where we would be working. In hindsight it was for the best and I feel like things happen for a reason, but definitely very stressful at the time!

What's the best piece of advice you've been given. What do you wish you'd know back when you started out?

Start small, don't take on too much! Do what you are passionate about and do it well. It is so much better to accomplish small goals well than to go big and do it half way. I don't know if we would do anything differently—it is a total learning experience every day and I feel like we wouldn't be where we are without making mistakes and taking risks. You don't know unless you try!

What are your hopes and dreams for Noon Design? Where would you like the business to be in 5 years time ?

We would love to be bi-coastal! Both our families are on the east coast, but our heart lies here in California. It would be amazing to have shops in both places forcing us to travel back and forth getting the best of both worlds. I'm sure Nora would like it so she had two days off!

Name: **Mark Williams & Ben Hickman**

Business: **Brainbox Candy**

Founded in: **September 2008**

Location: **Essex, UK**

Website: **www.brainboxcandy.com**

Brainbox Candy was founded by brothers-in-law Mark Williams and Ben Hickman. They make irreverent humour greeting cards, fridge magnets, gift wrap, coasters and other novelty products, and are based in Leigh-on-Sea in Essex, England.

What is your background, and how did the idea to start a greetings card company come about?

The idea for Brainbox Candy came from a shared love that Ben and I have for irreverent humour greeting cards. Although there are a few great companies in this area of the market, we felt that there was a significant gap where we could apply a fresh approach to this genre of card and create refreshingly different product. We found the choice for this type of card was quite limited and dominated by just a few companies.

When we started the company I was working as a consultant business analyst in London, and Ben was running a graphic design agency. I very quickly realized that to get any sort of foot-hold in what is a highly competitive market I would have to leap in feet first and give up my full time employment. This was a difficult decision financially as we didn't take any sort of wages for the first eighteen months, but it did enable us to gain significant momentum very quickly as the majority of new independent publishers have to juggle their new business and a job for the first year or two. This resulted in the business growing incredibly quickly, and perhaps the pressure of having no income helped to spur me on! Rightly or wrongly we designed some initial product and then exhibited at the Top Drawer trade show in London. Looking back we were not in any way ready, and had a mild panic when customers starting coming on the stand and placing orders! Once we returned from the show it was all hands on deck getting the cards printed and packed. Back then we packed the cards ourselves and there were countless late nights spent at home after working hours preparing orders. It was fun but not something that I miss!

There are tons of graphic designers and illustrators out there who dream of using their designs on a range of products—it's such a competitive market. What research did you do?

Our research was to look at what volume of target retailers there were in the UK for the sort of product that we envisaged making, as well as visiting trade shows and speaking to other publishers. What was wonderful was how open some of these publishers were in providing information about the industry, to a couple of complete strangers.

When you first started out, what were your aims?

We always believed that we could grow Brainbox Candy into a credible business, but of course there was no guarantee. We never set out to create a hobby business and we were determined to make it work. It was a real slog trying to break into a mature market with retailers big and small, especially with such a non-traditional product. However, thankfully once a few brave retailers bought into the product and we were seen at a few trade shows others quickly followed.

Please describe the space you work from, and how has this changed from when you started out?

We started off renting a small area in an office and within nine months this had grown to a larger share of the building, plus a vacant warehouse that was also located on the same site.

Are two minds really better than one? Are you glad you did this together rather than starting your own solo ventures?

Ben and I are brothers-in-law, so have known each other for many years. It certainly helps when there are two of you to bounce around ideas, planning, making the many decisions that you are faced with for all aspects of the business and especially for the many trade shows that we attend throughout the year!

You produce a large range of high quality greetings cards. Does this require a load of investment and a big print run for every single design? How did you start off, and how have you managed to upscale production as your business has grown?

We started off with about sixty designs and printed them digitally in very small runs for samples and initial orders. This was not very cost-effective, and in addition it meant that we were often chasing our tails in order to have enough stock, as orders came in on an ad-hoc basis. As soon as we could, we started litho printing the best designs in large quantities, and gradually moved away from digital. This did, and still does, require a lot more capital outlay and risk in terms of getting stuck with slower selling titles, however, in terms of margin and maintaining good stock levels we feel it is essential.

Discuss the challenges you faced getting into retailers as a new company?

We now supply our cards to circa 750 stores in the UK, which is a combination of chains, independent multiples, and independent stores. We use a combination of agents, trade shows and direct contact in order to win new business and garner repeat orders. Getting in with the larger retailers is sometimes not easy, as they are approached by hundreds of new publishers, so it is often just a case of perseverance and tenacity! If you are approaching a retailer, be realistic and ask yourself: do they stock the sort of product that you have? Send samples, follow up without hounding them, and then contact them when you release new product even if your previous attempts have failed.

> With greetings card being a fairly low value item, you must need to sell lots to make any profit. Do you have minimum orders for retailers in order to make all the admin of an order worthwhile?

We have minimum order of £100 for the independent retailers and on this sort of quantity we only make a small profit.

> Now that you are proper business people with lots of dull admin and paperwork to attend to, is it harder to keep the creative juices flowing? What happens when your "fun" becomes your job?

There certainly is a lot of admin to do with a growing business, however, we still just about have enough time to do the essential fun part of the business, which is creating new ranges and coming up with captions. A few trips to the pub normally help the creative juices to flow, and we can tell our wives it's for research purposes!

> Are you glad you started the business? With the benefit of hindsight, is there anything you'd do differently?

We are definitely glad that we have started the business. Seeing our product in shops still gives us both a big kick. Seeing your ideas realized on a product and knowing that it is bought by hundreds of thousands of people and making them laugh is amazing! Highlights include being finalists for the card industry Henries awards for the last two years running. I don't think there is anything we would have done differently, as we are delighted with the progress we have made thus far and the firm footing that we now have in the marketplace.

> Where would you like Brainbox Candy to be in 5 years time?

We see continued growth over the next five years in cards, gifts and novelties and we would like the brand to become well known and recognized by the public. We are pushing into new product areas to rollout the brand even further, and pushing into overseas markets following some initial successes.

> Words of wisdom! What sort of advice do you wish you had been given before you started out? Any tips for others?

- Don't expect it to be easy and make sure you have enough savings to see you through the early years.
- Don't give up, and deal with any rejections pragmatically and keep going.
- Be like a dog with a bone when you are chasing new business.
- Think differently, and go against the grain for new product if necessary.
- Customer service is paramount—look to exceed what your competitors are doing.
- Keep the product fresh—buyers always want to see new product.
- Expect to work harder than you have ever worked before!

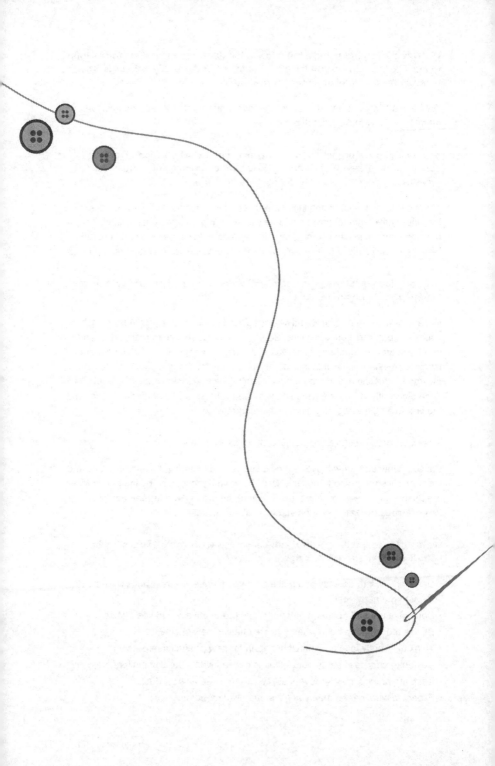

people will always need plates

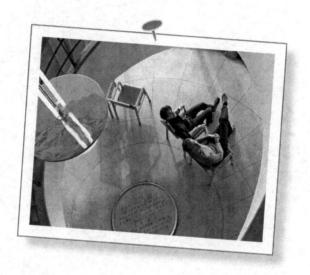

Name: **Hannah Dipper and Robin Farquhar**

Company Name: **People Will Always Need Plates**

Founded in: **2004**

Location: **Hertfordshire, UK**

Website: **www.peoplewillalwaysneedplates.co.uk**

People Will Always Need Plates is the creation of Hannah Dipper and Robin Farquhar.

Launched in 2004, they use high quality, low volume batch production to create witty, thoughtful and stylish products as a direct antithesis to the current proliferation of cheap, throwaway design. In keeping with their credo that good design should be used and enjoyed, treasured and shared, Hannah and Robin try to develop products that, while diverse in style and application, always retain the fundamental values of functionality and beauty.

Given their varied backgrounds (Hannah is an ex-RCA ceramist and has extensive industrial ceramics experience as well as work for Conran & Partners, while Robin, having studied industrial design at Brunel has spent most of his working life in exhibition and interior design agencies) they offer a complete product, graphic, exhibition and interior design service alongside their core range and commissioned wares.

Tell us a bit about your design/career backgrounds and how the idea for People Will Always Need Plates came about?

We've both worked extensively in-house and freelanced for a number of consultancies and agencies. People Will... was set up alongside other jobs as an outlet for own-designed products and batch production. The name is taken from the wonderful 1980s adverts for British Telecom starring Maureen Lipman. The sentiment rang true—especially for Hannah, whose education was in ceramics and glass!

How did you make the leap from working for other people to starting PWANP?

People Will Always Need Plates was the brand title of products designed by Hannah between 2000–2003, but was officially registered as a company by us in June 2004 when we started to collaborate on projects. The first project was born out of taking a stall at Scarlet Project's V&A Village Fete. We produced a set of 12 prototype platters featuring illustrations of domestic architecture in London that visitors had to put in chronological order, and the prize was a coloring book of the illustrations. The stall was an unexpected hit and buyers from the V&A shop approached us about stocking manufactured ware, and so People Will Always Need Plates in its plate-centric form as recognized today was born!

You produce a broad range of products—from ceramics (mugs, plates) to textiles (bags, purses, cushions)—how did you go about finding the right people to produce these for you?

People Will Always Need Plates was set up to produce ware to the best of our abilities using UK-based manufacturers wherever possible. Having worked for so many years in consultancies, where work can sometimes be an unbalanced slog of manufacturing costs over creativity, we were keen to retain as much creative freedom as possible and concentrate on subject matter and quality that we felt appropriate to the brand we were building. This has frequently been at the expense of profit, but the primary basis for the company has always been to produce what we believe to be interesting ideas, rather than making ware suitable for sale on the high street.

Finding the right people to make our work has taken a great deal of time and effort, and a lot of trial and error—there's no magic wand for this one, just clear briefing, realistic expectations and a lot of finger crossing!

That's a lot of stock! How do you store and distribute it all?

We're still a small company and do everything ourselves. Seven years in, and we're still subletting a dark damp space nearby and tend to pack orders either very early in the morning or on Sunday afternoons so that working hours are kept free.

On one hand, we dream of the day we can afford 'real' warehousing and help with distribution. On the other, it's therapeutic to pack orders, and a change from close work at the computer or chasing manufacturers. It's relatively uncomplicated and we rather enjoy the process of boxing china and sometimes adding freebies to orders for a splendid customer surprise!

Your products are stocked all over the world—how did you make the leap into supplying internationally?

International stockists have slowly approached us over the years. We never seem to find the time to make a good export plan. We work with Pop Corn on distribution in the Benelux countries, which is great—they take our work to trade fairs in France and take orders there, and then we ship a single pallet out to Paris where it's broken down into individual shop orders. It's really difficult to ship to America and Japan as bone china is so heavy and bulky—but our European orders are steadily increasing, not least in thanks to the strength of the Euro since 2009.

What was the first Trade Fair fair you showed at? What have been your experiences, from your very first show, right up until now?

Trade Fairs are, frankly, horrible. Days and days in a daylight-free, air-conditioned space, watching buyers walk past and really hoping they'll stop at your stand to chat. Our first trade show was Pulse in London in 2005. We were given a last-minute space with massive discount and thought it worth a try. In more recent times we've shown at Pulse and Top Drawer, and one year won space at 100% Design to exhibit our textile collaboration with Margo Selby. However, our work is quite niche (or geeky) and trade shows tend to lead to commissions for us, rather than large retail orders.

They are a useful tool to remind buyers that you're around, but we've never come out of a fair having made a decent profit. Direct selling shows are much better for us.

We LOVE meeting our customers as they're generally as geeky as us, so we get to gossip mightily about all things architectural and often receive suggestions for new work alongside selling current lines.

Selling to retailers—for the benefit of those not yet wholesaling, how do you calculate your wholesale price to retailers?

Our recommended retail prices are based on the wholesale price x 2, plus VAT. Thanks to weak Sterling at this time, our prices in Europe are easily achieved. In the UK, increased VAT means that the prices on our website are lower than those in shops. However, we figure that as customers to our shop have to pay P&P, we're not undercutting our retailers, which would be really rude. Larger retailers demand a much larger margin, and thanks to our high manufacturing costs, it's really difficult for us to meet their cost prices on small orders.

Discuss pros and cons of selling solely to the public vs. wholesaling to retailers?

Wholesaling is what makes our business viable—retailers account for a significant percentage of our sales and allow us the financial freedom to create ever greater numbers of designs and new products.

We sell to customers directly through our site and also at shows and fairs. As mentioned previously, we work really well at fairs—we love meeting our customers and they're often curious to talk to us about how we work and what we do. Feedback from customers is invaluable and of course the margin taken on direct sales is far more healthy. Like trade fairs, selling at shows can be costly, but we always do well and enjoy the experience, so to us, it's way more rewarding.

Please describe the space you work from—how has this changed from when you started out?

We work in a studio at the top of the house. The company started out in Robin's studio flat, so the luxury of a whole room is quite splendid! Sometimes we yearn for the luxury of more space and room to employ assistants and take interns, but we also have a young daughter and the benefit of working from home is that she sees lots of us both over the duration of the working week.

You are a couple, and have a small child and work from home. How do you manage to keep family and work life separate AND have time for the kids? Any tips for others in this position?

We went to a wonderful talk by a jeweler several years ago, where she talked about just this subject and pointed out that when you run a small business, that in itself is like a baby to you, so when you have a child as well, it's very hard to balance the needs of the two! We're immensely cautious about ensuring work time is separated from child time and Robin has inevitably become the chief of People Will... while Hannah assists with admin duties wherever possible and undertakes a lot of the freelance work.

We're fortunate that for two years, our daughter was super good at coming along to meetings and sitting quietly with a snack and toys. Occasionally, she still comes to help with packing—there's a lot of fun to be had in a space full of cardboard boxes, packing chips and huge quantities of bone china!

This occurs increasingly as time goes on—if you create work that is interesting, it inevitably consciously or unconsciously influences others. A lovely customer visited us at East London Design Show a couple of years ago brandishing what looked like one of our plates. It was actually a souvenir from a museum in Korea, flawlessly recreating our style—the customer was delighted by their discovery and it was strangely enthralling to see how far our style had spread. It can be more irritating when this occurs closer to home, but as a good designer, you move on and try new things. What's done is done.

Words of wisdom. What's the best piece of advice you've been given? Any advice for others thinking of doing their own thing?

Wisdom. We have so much to offer—and continue to learn daily how better to do things. Our top three tips or suggestions are:

New graduates should go and work in-house for someone else to learn about project management and the 'real world' before venturing out alone. This gives a fantastic understanding of design as business and better grounding from which to create ones own brand. See it as finishing school for design graduates.

Join craft organizations such as Hidden Art for access to affordable business advice and seminars/workshops, and take the opportunity to meet other designer-makers through networking events. Since establishing People Will... we've been members of Design Nation, Craft Central and Hidden Art and all three have given us amazing opportunities for learning and development.

Create a decent, simple, well-written website and a landline number. Potential customers are wary of mobile phone numbers, and generic email addresses can make you seem amateur and less convincing, even if your work is fabulous!

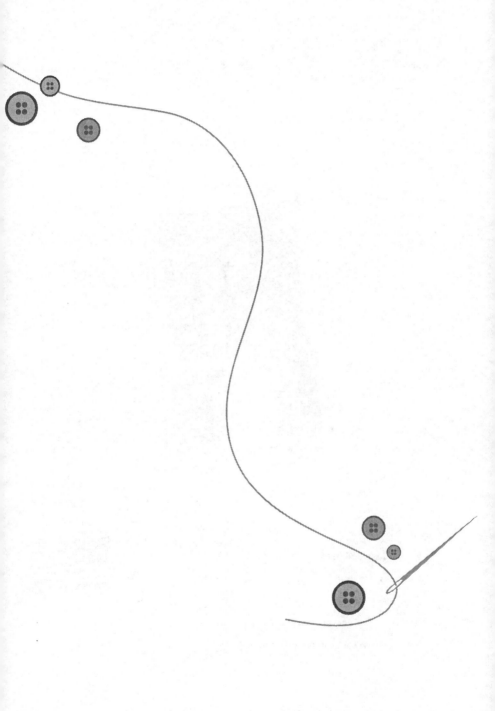

are you?^{tm}

Name: **Jessica Leale**

Business: **are you?**

Founded in: **2008**

Location: **New Jersey, USA**

Website: **www.areyoudesigns.com**

In 2008 Jessica Leale had the unique idea to offer a stylish and eco-friendly gift line with messages that are motivational, inspirational, and thought provoking. Jessica was influenced by everything around her and a desire to become more aware of the earth and how we interact with it—the world that we will leave to our children. She wanted to do something to inspire goodness, positive drive, encouragement, and love!

are you?™ products are richly designed, elegant, and fun. Brilliant jewelry and tasteful textiles exemplify the line. Each product is crafted with care and attention to detail, using only the finest, natural materials. With love and support from an amazing family and exceptional friends, Jessica started are you?™ hoping to be a catalyst for positive change. Her wish is that everyone will be inspired to celebrate life!

Tell us a little about are you?

are you™ is based out of my home in New Jersey. My company sells high-end, eco-friendly gifts that have either a motivational or inspirational question on each item, beginning with "are you". At this point, we have jewelry, stationery, soy candle and t-shirt lines. All items are made with high quality materials and are simple and stylish.

At the moment, I am working alone and working all areas of the business by myself. We are selling online (retail) and also to retail stores (wholesale). We are doing our first trade show next year in order to increase our visibility and sell to more retail locations.

Where did the idea for the business come from?

As silly as it sounds, the idea for are you™ literally popped into my head one night. I had been thinking about how bad news and negative stories dominate our media…I was aggravated by it, and ready to bring some positivity to our world.

Your range features great inspirational messages—are there any other creative brands or entrepreneurs that you admire?

I love many brands and like millions of others, I LOVE shopping. But the reason I created the line is because I was always looking for something like are you™ and I could never find it. I like style, simplicity, and meaning to a gift, and of course I try to be as green as possible. I felt like there was a void, and the more I thought about the idea, the more I thought my company could fill that void.

What did you do before you launched the company? Did you continue to work a job when you first started the business?

When I started my company, I was working part time at another company in the finance field. I have been lucky to have my husband working full time and to have the freedom to begin my company. To this day, because of the people and flexibility they give me, I have still not left my part time job!

Please describe the place you work from today—how does this differ to when you started out?

I started working from home, and I continue to do so. This allows me to save on rent and put more money back into the company.

With the day to day demands of running a business, how do you keep the creative juices flowing and find inspiration for each new collection?

As a small company, just starting out, I have the luxury of keeping the same products in production for some time. Most of my creative juices are used up these days on the marketing side! I am constantly trying to get product and brand awareness. In the future I know this will change, but by then, I will hopefully have other people working at the company and helping in the process.

Your range includes t-shirts, natural soy candles, jewelry and notecards—all with the same distinctive style and quality. How did you source the right suppliers?

I spent quite a lot of time finding my manufacturers for the different lines. I wanted each item to be made with quality, eco-friendly materials, and have a crisp simple look. I worked with a packaging/branding company to make sure that we kept the same look across every product line.

As a woman in business, how do you manage to keep family and work life separate AND have time for your family and yourself ?

I think the key is prioritization. My family has to come first, and then I try and keep a social life to have some fun! Because I work from home and for myself, I have the flexibility of working during the hours that everyone is out of the house and can "clock out" when I hear the bus coming around the corner! I have decided that I might not be as successful, or grow as quickly as other companies because of this, but it has been a choice that I am happy with.

Cashflow is always a difficult area—how do you stay afloat while growing your business?

Like many small companies, we have started off slowly and are excited for our future. We don't have any staff or a rent to pay, so we don't have many expenses. With marketing online and via phone calls and e-mails, we have been able to keep those costs down too. At this point we do not do any advertising, and we put all the money made with the company right back into it.

This has been a good 3 years for sure. I really love waking up every morning and working on my own company. The worst moments for me have been when I just have too much work, too little time and no other employees to delegate to. I have to do the work, no matter what, and do it right. I can have no excuses! The best moment so far has been my first sale to a retail store. The excitement they had for the line was similar to the excitement I have for the lines, and it was amazing to be there to witness the sale!

What's the best piece of advice you've been given?

I don't know that I was given much specific advice. I am an avid researcher, and have compiled years of tips from websites, books, interviews etc. Each is important in its own way, and each tip has been used at some point and in some situation. I was thoroughly prepared for opening my business. I did not want to regret my decision or get burnt out after a short time. I guess my advice to others would be to do the same! Going in blindly will not end well... know what you are in for and go for it 100%.

Jessica Leale's
Top Ten Tips for Creative Business Success!

1) Research everything there is to know about your product market, your competition and ideal customer.

2) Outsource at times when you need professional help and you cannot do it on your own.

3) Find things that keep you inspired.

4) Soak in any feedback and make adjustments accordingly.

5) Take a break every now and then in order to stay motivated for the long haul.

6) Find people and networks that can help you along the way, and don't be shy in helping others too!

7) Keep focused and stay true to the idea of your company. It is easy to get lost along the way.

8) Trust your instincts.

9) Make sure you love what you are doing and love your products. If you don't, the days will seem like 'work' and you will lose your drive.

10) Work hard!!

Hand Embroidered
Heirlooms of the Future

Name: Jan Constantine

Company Name: **Jan Constantine Ltd**

Founded in: **2002**

Location: **Cheshire, UK**

No. of Employees: **10 Full Time, 5 Part Time**

Website: **www.janconstantine.com**

Jan Constantine is a UK-based home-ware designer whose patriotic designs and bold motifs have become her signature and are stocked in hundreds of boutiques around the world.

Jan spent her early career as a successful fashion designer in London, UK. After 10 years she relocated to the Cheshire countryside and was inspired to move into interior design. Her homes have been featured in many prestigious home magazines and she has appeared on several TV shows, and she has also worked as a stylist on magazines such as Italian Vogue and W Magazine and various ad campaigns.

What began as a small business sewing lavender hearts around her kitchen table with friends quickly grew.

Her hand embroidery business has now grown into an established brand—today, Jan's designs are stocked in Liberty of London, Selfridges, Fortnum & Mason, Harrods and boutiques in Britain and the USA, with new product lines planned. In 2011 Jan's second book 'Love Stitching' was published in the UK by Jacqui Small and in the USA by Stash Books.

Tell us a bit about your design/career background, and how your company came about?

I used to make cushions for Christmas and birthday presents—everyone loved them and said I should go into business and sell them. I originally started my business around the kitchen table stitching lavender bags with friends, with the odd bottle of wine. I was known for my embellished and embroidered designs when I was in the fashion industry and I carried this over to the designs for my cushions and lavender hearts.

Your cushions and textiles are hand embroidered and you're a strong supporter of preserving these traditional skills. Tell us about how your products are made, and how did you find your very talented workforce?

I soon realized that if I was to be successful then I would have to have my designs made abroad. Although some of my products are made in the UK there is only a very limited number of hand-embroiderers here, so I had to make several trips to India to find the right people to work for me. My products are made using traditional skills that are passed from father to son over the generations. We work mainly with a company that interprets what I need using natural fabrics and old fashioned stitching techniques. I went through at least half a dozen factories until I found the one I needed to interpret ideas and high quality.

Your HQ is based in the Cheshire countryside. Sounds idyllic! Describe to us your workplace now, and how this differs to when you first started out?

When I first started it was on the kitchen table at home, sewing with a few friends. Then we moved into an old renovated stable block. Now we work from two offices, one in the stable block which is near to my house and one at a warehouse about 5 miles away, where we now pack and dispatch.

You also design ceramics, stationery, nightwear etc. Who manufactures these for you?

We had a disaster with the first ceramics company not being able to fulfill orders and demand. We now have a licensing program that we are developing with specialist companies that produce stationery, textiles, candles, bed linen and gift wrap etc. I found it was very trial and error to begin with but now I have consultants to help me.

With such a wide range of products, that's a lot of stock! How do you store and distribute it all? Do you use a fulfillment warehouse? Do you still ship all your own orders?

We ship all our own orders for our core product from our warehouse. Our licensed products are dispatched from the licensee's warehouse to the trade accounts (we just deal with our web orders and exhibition stock). Stock can be a nightmare if you don't control it properly. Regular stock counts and clear outs should be routine. I try to 'throw out' old lines when I introduce new ones to keep stock down but I'm constantly being asked for my archive numbers to be revived by stores, so this can be tricky. In future I would like to change to a fulfillment house as there are so many overheads with our own warehouse and the business is changing the way it works.

Your products are stocked all over the world—how did you make the leap from supplying to UK shops into supplying internationally?

My Local Chamber of Commerce and the DTI (Department for Trade and Industry) helped us by offering workshops, expert advice and grants. WIRE (Women in Rural Enterprise) were also helpful to us in the early days of the business. You must endeavor to establish in your own country first and foremost. The New York International Gift Fair was a great platform for us to test the US market, and then sheer determination!

Trade Fairs—an expensive, but necessary tool?

Very expensive, but essential for marketing as well as sales. It is great to be able to launch your new collections and it makes you focus on a deadline. You can display your products how you want the world to see them, keep in touch with buyers and network with other exhibitors and press.

The Spirit of Christmas Fair in London was the first consumer fair I did, and I launched my business there. It wasn't an instant success but I wasn't deterred. My next fair was the UK Trade Show Top Drawer a year later when I was ready to supply trade, and my products were very well received.

A couple of fairs later the Bed and Bath buyer from the famous London store Fortnum and Mason placed an order right on my stand. I was over the moon when she told me who she was—my first London store!

At the next fair I did—The Country Living Fair—the first person on my stand was a buyer from Liberty of London and I nearly fell through the floor! I always loved Liberty, as a student I would spend hours mulling over which print I should spend my allowance on. My English Country Garden designs were on their shelves within weeks! My products still sell in Fortnum & Mason and Liberty today.

The worst exhibition that I ever did was a brand new one at Excel in London's Docklands. It looked great but was an utter disaster. I lost lots of money because there were hardly any people there and they had no money to spend. I wasn't the only person to shed a tear that week—it was so disappointing. I'm very cautious now about new fairs that aren't tried and tested. Even established ones, I always check out by walking the floor and getting feedback from several companies prior to booking anything that I haven't tried before.

In the early days I used to stay up most of the night preparing price lists and press packs. I used to be so nervous on the stand and it took several shows before I had enough confidence to approach buyers to ask if they needed help—I was terrified! I used to find the first day of a show absolutely exhausting—after putting together a new collection, driving down to London, setting up the stand myself and then presenting the collection and myself as poised as possible, I was wiped out! But it has all paid off, and now I have staff to do this for/with me.

Some exhibition organizers are very kind and offer free exhibitor drinks at the end of the first day and sometimes have an award ceremony for best stand in show etc. I always think how great it must be for new exhibitors to win a prize —so encouraging for new start-ups.

Selling to retailers—for the benefit of those not yet wholesaling, how do you calculate your wholesale price to retailers?

I started off as a retail business selling to the consumer so when I started being asked for trade prices I had to do a rethink. Basically I work out exactly what it costs to produce something, have it delivered to me and finished/handled in-house, I then double the price and add on VAT to calculate my trade price. The trade then do the same thing (double it) to get the retail price. This doesn't apply to every customer and every product though—but it's how I started. If I have a very large order I can reduce the price if I can get the components cheaper. Some large UK department store chains do work on a higher mark-up than most, but I'm not always in a position to facilitate that due to the nature of my hand embroidery. It would be different if my products were all made by machine, but my products are more people based.

Cash-flow—one of the biggest challenges of a small business owner. How have you financed the growth of your company?

I began with a family loan of £10,000. Soon when I needed more, I had 2 repeats of that. A short time after, I had two loans from my home mortgage company. I then increased the mortgage on my London crash pad, but then had to rent it out to make the payments. Then I needed to put a lot of money into the business so I pitched to investors who now own 35% of my business after a further investment. A couple of years ago, I had a massive bank loan to help me with the next stage of growth. I've often paid for shows and shipments with my personal credit cards.

To keep on top of the late payments I have a rotweiller called Liz who calls everyone as soon as she sniffs anything overdue and continues to do so! We send a formal letter initially, then a second to warn that we will be taking them to court if they don't pay. We have always been paid except when a famous London store went bust. They started up again in business but we didn't have a chance of recouping our loss. Luckily we put lots of pressure on them prior to them folding and we did get some payment but not all so it pays off to be vigilant. All new accounts I keep on pro forma payment for at least a year or until they spend a certain amount of money with us. Obviously large stores won't pay pro forma, but I don't allow anybody over 30 days. A small company cannot handle 60 days or more.

You've now launched your second book (*Love Stitching*, the follow-up to the fabulous 2008's *Heirloom Embroidery*). So you must be rich, right?

No—not yet! When I struck the first deal with my publisher she said to me "It won't buy you a house in France" and so far I don't have the money to get that house (in Italy actually). Every spare penny I have goes straight back into the business. It may be successful but it is also very expensive to run.

I received an email from Jacqui Small saying that she'd seen my very lovely work in Liberty and asking if I would be interested in talking about writing a book. I'm thrilled to have just launched my second book. The advances that I have received from my book deals have been treated as my bonus and nothing to do with the business, so I have actually used them for treats for me and my family. You only make lots of money from writing books if they sell very well. You don't see many craft books in the top 100! But you never know! I would always say it's great to have the chance to write a book because it gives you credibility and it makes you the expert in your field.

Your designs are incredibly unique and are instantly recognizable as a "Jan Constantine". How does it feel when obvious copies start springing up on the high street. What have been your experiences of copyright infringement?

I have been copied and passed off by large and small companies and even department stores who you wouldn't dream of—because they like to appear squeaky clean. In my eyes it's stealing, because my designs are so unique, it's so obvious when they're copied.

I'm currently in process of trying to stop a huge high street chain from killing off one of my most successful pieces. I was made aware of it in a press pack from a magazine stylist and we're trying to stop it reaching the shelves. We managed to put a stop to it thanks to the early tip off. I'm a member of ACID (Anti Copying in Design —a UK based organization that works with designers to protect their interests), but quite honestly the cost of using even their discounted lawyer is prohibitive for small companies and designers to go after the big boys.

With the help of one of my consultants I sent a letter pointing out breach of copyright and threatening legal action. The small companies often ignore it and say they've done nothing wrong and it's their own design!! That's when you have to go legal— but if you can make an example of someone, word gets round and others are less likely to copy you. It isn't easy but we have to make a point.

Words of wisdom...What's the best advice you've been given? What do you wish you'd known back when you started out?

I know it's not probably what I should be saying but if I knew how much money, blood, sweat and tears I would go through before I began my business, I don't think I would have done it!

I have had big problems with people that have worked alongside me too. I'd say be careful with partners or anyone who wants to get into your company—try to remain independent if you can and get the best advice you can afford without compromising your position or business. Power can be a very dangerous thing and when some people see success they want a part of it.

People have advised me all the way and some has been good and some has been bad. In retrospect, if I could do it all again I would have more confidence in myself and not trust certain people so much! As a company grows it's good to learn about shares and investments before they happen—because it can be a can of worms! And if you don't know your stuff and you have an attractive business, you'll be eaten alive by those who want a stake in your business.

The best advice for me is to listen to my gut instinct! If a crisis is happening, it is best for me to get away, to think logically and not to panic—get some good advice from a calm person, not a pessimist. My naivety has cost me a lot of wasted money, effort and time. The best advice has been from people who are impartial and not connected with the business at all.

For the future, the business model is changing. My brand is strong enough now to be licensed into many different products. This is the most exciting thing I have ever done. It is so amazing to see my designs come to market without having to produce them and sell them myself!

My stationery and tin-wear launched recently and it has already sold double what was expected! I love the fact that anyone will be able to buy into the Jan Constantine brand because it's affordable. We've got bags, kitchen textiles, melamine and bed linen in the pipeline and already have china, greeting cards, gift wrap, gift tags and boxes. It's an exciting time!

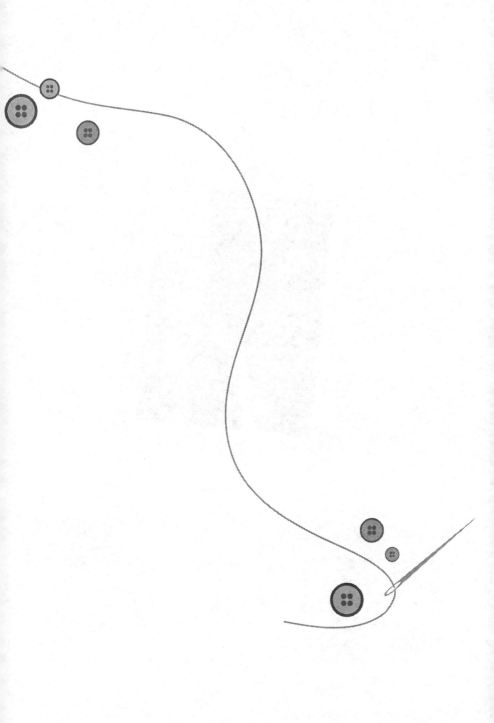

dbO
HOME

Name: **Dana Brandwein Oates**

Company Name: **dbO Home**

Founded in: **2005**

Location: **Litchfield County, CT, USA**

No. of Employees: **1**

Website: **www.dbohome.com**

Dana Brandwein Oates founded dbO Home in 2005 after spending nearly 20 years in the music business. Having left NYC for Litchfield County, her vision was to create a collection of unique homewares for a bit of luxury everyday —a soothing mix of tactile textures, natural materials and earthy hues created by hand. The dbO Home collection is anchored with the ceramics made one by one in a studio overlooking a spectacular view of the wetlands in bucolic Sharon, Connecticut.

When Dana's husband Daniel Oates joined in collaboration, the vision really started to come together. An acclaimed sculptor and toy designer, he adds a distinct look to their wood and porcelain accessories and lighting, as well as his bespoke furniture which is painstakingly crafted from highly figured woods in the big red barn across from their ceramic studio.

Textiles were a natural addition to soften the range, and Dana and Daniel were thrilled to find artisans that could make their designs come to life. The dbO Home line reflects the natural beauty of their surroundings while maintaining a bit of the urban edge of the city Dana and Daniel called home for so long.

Please describe dbO Home as it stands today?

I don't have far to get to work which is quite nice! The dbO Home ceramic studio is attached to my home and the woodshop is located in our barn. Danny and I are now a creative partnership and while we work in separate studios we come together for meetings over lunch and walking our two dogs. We have one full time employee who has learned all aspects of production, except for wheel throwing. I work with another local artisan to produce our wheel thrown pieces. We make almost all of our products in our studios, but we have recently launched a line that we designed and are having handcrafted for us at a workshop in Peru, and we are currently looking for ways to expand our line and production outside of our studios while keeping our style and quality.

dbO Home was launched in 2005 as a website offering my one-of-a-kind ceramics, but it became clear to me after attempting to secure some press attention that I needed to develop a line that I could make in multiples. I sold a small collection to some trendsetting shops in NY and Chicago in the spring of 2006, and having those clients helped me get juried in to the Handmade Division of the NY International Gift Fair in January 2007—that's when dbO Home launched a wholesale collection. We sell our line to high to end shops across the US and we also do custom hospitality work. Clients include ABC Home & Carpet, Bergdorf Goodman, Barneys, Aero, Lekker Home, Gumps, Velocity Art And Design, Blue Hill At Stone Barns, ABC Kitchen and Commis.

You spent 20 years in the music industry before launching dbO home. Where did the idea for the business come from?

I was never a crafter but I had a very passionate interest in interior and product design. I was certainly a collector and an admirer...I collected mid-century ceramics (mostly American) and admired contemporary designers like KleinReid, Tom Dixon and Clarisse Hulse. At some point in my music career I was longing to be a designer of some sort, but had no idea how I could make that happen. I knew that I had the best possible job for me at a record label but it wasn't fitting me as well as it used to and I needed a change. When my label, Elektra, merged into Atlantic Records I was given a big push to figure it out. It was an opportunity to make a change, and in all honesty I had no idea what I was going to do and it took quite a bit of push from my family and friends to take the leap. I was all over the place in my head...I had a stationery piece I spent months designing and researching manufacturing, I applied for stylist jobs and a food magazine job, I thought of going to school to get an interior designer degree...I had to make a choice. After selling some of my ceramics in a "sample sale" in my apartment I decided to start dbO Home with ceramics with the hopes to expand to all sorts of objects.

Please describe the place you work from today—how does this differ to when you started out?

I have a fairly well equipped ceramic studio and home office—and my husband Danny has a woodshop and his own home office. The studio has two rooms—we do our handbuilding, slipcasting, clay reclaiming and shipping from one room and sand, glaze and fire our work in the other. It's not fancy, but it's functional... shiplap walls, cement floors, work tables running along two sides with a big slab roller in the middle and a pugmill at one end. We have 4 kilns—three front loaders and one top loader (my original kiln). And one electric potter's wheel. I started with my wheel upstairs in my house in a room not yet renovated. I had to go down stairs for water and try really hard not to spill the water as I headed down a spiral staircase! I fired my work at my teacher's studio and glazed it there too. Happily the spiral staircase is gone and running water is in the glaze room. Danny's woodshop has all kinds of machinery and the steamer he created to steam bend the legs of our tables and cake stands...his space is much bigger, but mine has heat!

With the day to day demands of running a business, how do you keep the creative juices flowing and find inspiration for each new collection?

There are times when the minutiae of running a business gets in the way of inspiration, but I am always thinking of new things I want to make or design and have made. I am a magazine junkie and pore over design and food mags daily (re-reading old issues) looking for the way a stylist put things together, or color palettes, textures, that sort of thing. I'd like to have more time to just work out new ideas or to visit museums, shops etc....but the orders have to be filled and the non-creative jobs have to be done too!

Yes, expensive, but yes, necessary. And yes exhausting! My first show was NYIGF in January of 2007 and I was petrified! I had walked the show a number of times but I never did so much as a crafts fair before heading in to the mouth of the monster! Danny helped me a great deal designing the booth. And a decorator friend helped me merchandise it so that my work stood out. Loading in was a disaster.

Rule number one—don't follow the rules! We read the guidelines and followed them—so we did not have a dolly or hand-truck, though we loaded ourselves in to the show. We were told to park at the furthest end of Jacob Javits Center as you could get from my booth...it was January and freezing. We hand carried all of our shelving, samples, rug, curtains etc...what was about 4 city blocks in the winter cold. It took about 3 weeks of massage therapy to put me back together! My pricing was way too low. I thought I was very clever in collecting Terms from other vendors the last time I walked the show...so I picked my favorite and chose to add a 20% handling charge on to shipping. Not my best idea as was pointed out by one of my first clients. But all in all—it was a good show. I am not an aggressive sales person but I did alright and learned a great deal from that first show including to raise my prices, include the costs of handling into the wholesale pricing and under no circumstance come to the show without a hand truck!!

Dealing with buyers is interesting. You have to be confident in your work, and know your capabilities. Some buyers are very decisive. Some want your help to pull together a group that will work in their store. And all buyers shopping for handmade work are looking for something unique—so you must be familiar with where you sell your work because you don't want to sell to the shop across the street—not good for the buyer and ultimately not good for you. You may have to turn away a customer or two—or interest them in an alternative collection, but it's important to not overlap.

With each show I learned more and more, both from my experience with buyers and talking to other vendors. I developed some great friendships doing NYIGF over the past few years and so many people have helped me.

We now also do the Architectural Digest Home Design Show which is entirely different as it is directed towards the trade and the public. We focus on furniture and home accessories at that show and we set up a more curated booth. We intend to add a few more shows to open ourselves up to new markets. But yes, they are a large expense so we need to determine the best possibilities—and I always walk a show before deciding to exhibit.

If doing a trade show is too much to start with, I really suggest picking out a few key shops that you feel your work suits and then sending a concise but informative and friendly email with some images of your work to the buyer. Offer to come show your work if they are interested, or send samples if you wish. That's how I got those first few stores. And I still send emails like this to buyers I have not had the opportunity to meet at the shows.

Shipping ceramics to stores and customers must be tricky—fragile yet heavy, therefore expensive. How does this affect your ability to sell to retailers across the country?

Again, this took a lot of trial and error but I finally found a great packing material–Geami–that is cost effective because I do not need bubble wrap and paper. It takes less time to pack and it's green. I use double thick boxes rather than a box inside a box and make sure to pack tightly…you don't want anything moving around and I fill with newsprint. It's been working very well. There are less breaks, it costs less and the material is not offensive and can be reused as fill. I ship with UPS—and keep boxes within the normal size box range. So the shipping costs aren't crazy. And I incorporate the costs of the packing materials and time it takes to pack within the wholesale price. Now shipping our furniture is a whole other story along with shipping outside the US. We're still working on getting the costs down there.

You now have a range of textiles, produced by hand by artisans in Peru. How did you go about finding the right people to work with, and how do you maintain quality control?

I was really lucky and was asked to attend a trade show in Lima to meet different manufacturers. The folks that invited me had a good idea of what I was looking to do so they could set up meetings for me with the best possible manufacturers. The textile line was totally new to me, but my mother is a textile designer. She came with me to Lima and helped me ask the right questions so that I could come away with an idea of what I wanted to try. The manufacturers I work with have a very high level of quality and do work for some very high end designers and bigger companies—I was confident I was working with the right people from our initial meetings.

As a woman in business, how do you manage to keep family and work life separate *AND* have time for your husband / yourself / a social life?!

It's not easy to stop working. And Danny and I work together, so it takes extra effort to make time for each other that doesn't involve work. But we make the effort. We don't have kids but we do have two very demanding dogs. They make us have to stop for breaks to tend to their needs—one is extremely vocal. I had a marketing position for a record label for almost two decades. In that job I worked all day and had to go out many evenings to see bands and go to dinners…it took an effort to have a social life then as well (though my job was very social by its nature). I would say, make it part of your job to take time for yourself, your family, your friends….work hard, but take the time away from the work. It will only make you better at what you do.

I am going to cheat here and give you a few best moments because I cannot choose!

The first was the moment the buyer from ABC Carpet & Home said I would be their new vendor. It was a whirlwind moment....a group of people going through the items, writing things down, putting pieces together...my business changed dramatically that day!

The second was when the manager of Blue Hill at Stone Barns contacted me about some samples—being a foodie and very familiar with Chef Dan Barber I was floored to have the opportunity to have him look at my work for this amazing restaurant. This became a collaboration with some incredibly talented people, and we now make them custom plates, vases, platters and more.

And the third stand out best moment was when West Elm asked me if would be interested in designing for them. It was a moment of pure validation.

The worst moment...hmmm...it really hasn't been that bad, but the worst thing that has happened was having my neighbor try to shut us down! It's a very long story, so here's my tip, make sure that if you have a home business you work with your town to have everything set up within your town's rules and regulations. Then if an ornery neighbor should try to destroy everything you have been working for—you will be prepared. We won the battle, but it was very stressful .

Value your work. Determine what you want your lifestyle to be—then create your business model to suit your lifestyle. These are two pieces of advice given to me by a friend who has a very successful business and loves her work. And I always think of her when I need to get business focused.

dbO Home is growing. We are working towards having a line produced outside our studio—we've done the first pieces of dbO WARE and look forward to doing more. There will be another collection with West Elm, and we will be focusing even more on furniture and lighting. Exciting times!

Dimbleby Ceramics

Name: **Mathew and Rachel Dimbleby**

Company Name: **Dimbleby Ceramics**

Founded in: **2011**

Location: **Stoke-on-Trent, Staffordshire, UK**

Website: **www.dimblebyceramics.co.uk / www.daisydimbleby.com**

Dimbleby Ceramics are based in Staffordshire, England in the heart of the area historically known as "The Potteries".

Founded in 2011 by husband and wife team Matthew and Rachel Dimbleby, their products are high end gift ware made from locally sourced ceramic materials.

After working in the local pottery industry for 5 years, Mathew studied Ceramic design at Staffordshire University which led him to supplying large stores like John Lewis, Dickens and Jones and Heals of London with contemporary ceramics. He has won the Whittard of Chelsea award for the most innovative and commercially viable product and achieved a merit in the Shell Livewire awards, has a wealth of knowledge on traditional ceramic making techniques and is a talented thrower.

Rachel studied Surface Pattern Design at Staffordshire University and has taught Art and Design at school, college and university level. She is also a freelance card designer for leading craft magazines. Rachel adds the all important finishing touches to the company's gorgeous gifts.

Please tell us a little about Dimbleby Ceramics, the company?

The company is run by myself and my wife Rachel—we are both trained designers, and our studio is based in Stoke-on-Trent, Staffordshire, England. We design and make a range of earthenware products which include teapots, cream and milk jugs, mugs and hand thrown bowls all of which carry the signature heart or star hand applied raised motif.

As well as making hollowware, we also create beautiful ceramic hangings, finished with beautiful ribbon—from a local manufacturer who has been making ribbon since the 1800's—then finished with a charm style bead. All the work that we produce can be personalized for that special occasion.

What is your background, and what were you doing before you launched the company? Where did the idea for Dimbleby Ceramics come from?

I worked in the industry when I left school at 16 for a company called J.W Hand and Partner, and it was here that I was able to experience all of the skills required to take a product from a design idea into a model and then into the making or production stage.

I stayed with the company for five years and then went on to work in glass for a further three years. After eight years in the industry I started to draw again in my spare time and realized that my real passion lay in design. I then embarked on a Foundation Art & Design course at Staffordshire University and then went on to Study BA Hons Design and Ceramics. On completion of the course I attended New Designers at the Islington Business Design Centre. This created a real platform for me to launch as a designer maker, enabling me to run the business for a further three years designing and making for companies such as Heals of London and John Lewis amongst others.

It was at this point that my family grew and with two small children to support I went into teaching. This enabled me to still engage in ceramics and art but in very challenging environments. My first three years were spent teaching adults who were sectioned under the mental health act. The next nine years saw me move into teaching in a category B prison and eventually become the Learning and Skills Manager responsible for all the education delivery.

When the opportunity for redundancy arose, I decided that I would have a change of direction and go back to what I was passionate about, clay and design. With all my previous knowledge and skills I launched Dimbleby Ceramics with the support and design input of my wife, Rachel. The emphasis would be on creating high quality products at a competitive price.

Please describe the place you work from today—how does this differ to when you started out?

When I first started out in the 1990's, I rented a studio. The only down side to this was the ever increasing overheads and the lack of access for visitors. Rachel and I then bought our first house and had enough land to build our first studio. The advantage of this was no travel costs to get to work and lower overheads. There are those who say that the only disadvantage is you are never away from work which is partly true! The real advantage is you can set your own working pattern, you can have a day off in the week if you need to, and work weekends—offering flexibility if you have a growing family.

Our current studio is based in Stoke-on-Trent as we are passionate about keeping ceramics alive, especially as the area has lost much of its manufacturing heritage.

Matthew—you have won a Whittard of Chelsea award for the most innovative and commercially viable product—please tell us a bit about that?

This Award was won when I first started up some years ago, however it was good to have my products recognized. The Princes Trust charity initially helped me with a small grant when I very first started up, and I had a stand at the Autumn Fair trade show at the Birmingham NEC with their support. This led to me more recently being a business mentor for the Trust. To be able to put something back, as a mark of thanks because the work the Trust do is really important in supporting other young businesses as they develop.

Many artists and potters dream of turning their creative talents into a living, but often find the reality of producing items in volume, running a business and striving to earn enough can be just as confining as a regular job. What has been your experience of turning your art into a viable commercial business?

It is important to understand costings from the outset—your time, raw materials and firing costs. It is then essential to research your market, research what other products are out there and for what price. What is your unique selling point that puts you ahead of the competition? Is the product viable, will it make enough profit for you? Sometimes products are not viable due to the way they are made, so you may have to rethink what you are going to take into the market place. When you start out in business you may need to do other part time work as much of your money will be invested back into the business doing trade fairs and advertising to build up a solid customer base. My wife and I do a job share with each of us teaching two days each a week—this does however mean that we often work weekends to keep on top of orders.

If you think that setting up in business is an easy option then think again, it takes lots of hard work, dedication and passion and the ability to take knock backs and keep pushing forward.

If you do not believe in your products no one else will, as the passion will not come over when you speak to potential clients.

You will be the designer, maker, marketing manager, accountant and point of call for everything. The good news is it gets easier as you become more familiar with the process and learn from mistakes you make as you develop.

What stores now stock your products? How did you achieve this?

We have about forty stockists of our products, from Devon to Glasgow and also Ireland. We initially achieved this by getting out and visiting shops that we knew were suitable for the products that we produce. We also do selected trade fairs such as Top Drawer at Earl's Court London and Harrogate Home & Gift show. My top tip would be do some self marketing to begin with, to see what the response is to your products before you spend big money on trade fairs. Most of all know where your products sit in the market place—low, middle or high end, and research the right shops. Much of this can be done online before you arrange to visit them. Oh and don't be afraid to pop in to shops speculatively, we have achieved many new accounts this way. You can leave a business card or just take some smaller sample products with you.

Your products all made by hand. Do you do this yourself, or outsource?

We make all the earthenware products ourselves but buy in the fine bone china from a local company and put our own designs on them.

In the current climate, what do you think are the biggest challenges you (and others) face as a designer/maker who wants to make a living from their craft?

The most challenging aspect in the current economic climate is to be able to offer products that cover a range of price points. Our products retail from approximately £4.50–£50. Be realistic with your pricing. At University many students are told that they can sell their work for hundreds of pounds, the reality of this is if you over price your products you won't sell enough to making a living from it. One of the biggest things some Universities appear to lack is teaching students on craft or design based courses realistic business knowledge.

What were your aims when you first started the business? Have you achieved those?

The aim in the first year was to have developed a substantial customer base and to be generating multiple reorders, as this is the real indicator that your product and its place in the market is right. So far we have achieved our objectives and we are approaching our second year of trading in a very tight economy.

Highs and Lows—Please describe the absolute stand-out best moment of your journey so far? And the worst?

The standout best moment was when we got our first order after developing a prototype and taking it through into a viable product that retailers wanted in their stores. The worst moment was when the kiln failed and we lost a whole batch of work—when this happens it is frustrating but you just start again and make sure the goods go out on time. If there is going to be any delay always ring your customer to let them know well in advance and the reason why.

Are you glad you started Dimbleby? With hindsight, what would you do differently?

We are 100% satisfied that we started Dimbleby Ceramics, and the first year has been really successful. The beauty of running your own business is the flexibility it offers, and knowing that all the hard work that we put in is for the family. The next year we will be focusing on and building brand awareness and our company name. I guess I made most of the mistakes the first time around when I set up as a designer maker in 1997 and I have put all this knowledge into practice, and building the business in methodical way.

Words of wisdom. What's the best piece of advice you've been given?

Best piece of advice is to know your market and your competitors. Invest wisely to maximize growth, ensuring you put money back into building the company and customer base, such as doing trade fairs. There is nothing that I would do differently, as I believe we approached everything in the right way this time.

Where would you like the company to be in 5 years time?

I would like us to have a small factory where we can make the products, employ staff and run educational linked activities with the emphasis on practical clay skills. Most of all, working with other companies and educational organizations to put the Pot back into the Potteries and to keep the tradition of ceramics alive in Stoke-on-Trent!

What does the future hold for you and the company...any exciting plans you'd like to share?

At the moment we are just focusing on building our name in the market place, and constantly designing and developing new products to add to our range. We have however just launched our first retail site and this is proving to be a real hit with customers old and new!

Matthew Dimbleby's
Top Ten Tips for Creative Business Success

1) Understand the market you are going into.

2) Who are your competitors and what are their prices, how do you compare?

3) What is your unique selling point, what makes you different to your competitors?

4) Understand your costings and what the different companies mark their products up at.

5) Be realistic with your prices.

6) Keep overheads as low as possible, start from home initially if you can.

7) Always be professional, know your products inside out, be passionate about what you do. If you aren't no one else will be!

8) Send information to relevant newspapers and magazines with images, this is a good way to get free exposure.

9) Get out on the high street and do some self marketing; this will also inform you if your product is viable.

10) Always rectify any mistakes immediately, it can take a long time to build up a working relationship with a customer or client, but can take one bad experience to lose them.

Name: **Doug Collum**

Company Name: **Stick Candles**

Founded in: **2009**

Location: **Old Forge, New York, USA**

Number of Employees: **8**

Website: **www.stickcandles.com**

Stick Candles are the creation of Douglas Collum, and what began as a simple task—to find a birthday gift for his nature-loving mother—evolved into a labor of love that resulted in the creation of this unique business.

Now based in The Old Forge—a beautifully restored property in the Adirondack Park in New York state—Doug creates and sells a beautiful range of handmade beeswax candles, cast from trees.

Tell us a bit about Stick Candles and how the idea came about?

Stick Candles started out as a gift for my mother, Barbara Collum, who is a designer/decorator and nature fanatic. She had been given a set of candles shaped like sticks and twigs, and loved them so much that she waited forever to burn them. When the time came to replace them, the source was no longer available.

I was working in Los Angeles as a Production Designer, and had a great team of shoppers and decorators ready for the task. We scoured the world and found nothing to match her expectation. There were all kinds of "artist's interpretations" but nothing cast directly from sticks and twigs. And none of those were beeswax, which was a must.

After exhausting all sourcing efforts I took the job to my prop fabrication shops and set construction companies. That effort produced multiple beautiful examples of cast candles, but none burned well for much longer than the length of a camera shot. So we threw in the towel. But it drove me mad to give up on something that seemed so simple in concept!

Time passed, Christmas was coming around again, and I decided that I would make the candles myself. The only way to develop a properly burning candle is to make it, light it, and watch it burn. Over and over and over!

I missed Christmas that year as well, and it wasn't until just after Mother's Day—nearly five months later—that I was able to send her a box of Stick Candles that were cast from real tree branches, made from beeswax.

It was not a business idea, until the combination of time and money already spent after the goal made it nearly a necessity to try and recoup costs. I sent a box of 50 pairs of candles to a friend who had just opened a small gift shop in Vermont. They sold out in a little over a week and they placed our first "real" order.

Describe the early days—from having the initial idea to launching the business?

Stick Candles as a business concept was somewhat reverse-engineered. I enjoyed my life in California, and the excitement of working on television and film sets. At the same time, the business climate was changing radically in terms of economics and technology.

I had the good fortune of working independently. So when film projects were not available I was able to spend more time on the candles. Finally I was able to pursue the candles full time.

Many designers find the business part of starting a business challenging. Did you have to do a business plan? Raise start-up capital?

I made a business plan with the help of friends and family, and eventually took a small business class at a Community College which put me in touch with mentors and other individuals facing the same challenges.

Originally the business was meant to grow on its own capital, but we did need a loan—and ultimately we will need another one to grow again.

You spent over 15 years in Los Angeles as a Production Designer in Film & TV— and now you make candles! Quite a change!

I thought I was going to be a rock star, a sculptor, or a writer! The more I pursued each dream, the more I understood the reality of each dream, though I still go for it everyday in music, art, and writing.

The Candles are a pretty good mix of pleasure and business. I find that aspects of all my real passions have contributed to this effort. I had certainly hoped to do something creative, and still do.

Do you make every single piece yourself, or employ help now? How has this changed from when you started out?

The process is still evolving. At first the degree of difficulty in each process was such that I really couldn't explain everything to someone else. I soon realized that in order to bring other people in, every process would have to be "designed" so that it was a simple as possible, yet without reducing it to hard, thoughtless labor.

We're still in the process of sorting out all of the legality of a fully-fledged workforce. So much of what has developed has been along the lines of part-time helpers, and out of work artists popping in here and there.

The key going forward is to examine every aspect of the production of the candles and working forward and backward from there, so that there is a workflow that is easy but not mind numbing, that will go all the way back through to the supply chain and all the way forward to creating new products and getting them to the right markets.

And I still haven't realized that I can't do everything myself!

Are Stick Candles stocked in any retailers? If so, how many, and how did you get them into stores? Do you do trade shows, or approach stores directly?

We're in over 25 retail stores, including Museum gift shops and Florists. Most of it is word of mouth. People who like our candles really like them and want to share them and that means with friends, and with their favorite local shops. We're starting to get random leads out of nowhere, but for the most part it's customers who are really excited about the product and want to share, which is great! We will be doing our first trade shows this year though, and I'm excited about that!

Please describe the space you work from. How has this changed from when you started out?

Stick Candles is in a circa 1940's building in Old Forge NY which is in the Adirondack Park. The building had been abandoned for over 8 years and it was listed for sale on the real estate market basically for the land only. It was thought that the building would be torn down.

We were able to negotiate an option to purchase the building and property in exchange for the expansive renovation. It is great, because it is really the heart's home for Stick Candles and every aspect of the choice to be in that location is positive and makes sense both for us and for the community.

It does have drawbacks however: we ran out of time and money for insulation and heating, so we will have to close for the winter this year and open back up in the late Spring. But from a branding and identity viewpoint, we couldn't ask for anything more. Prior to taking on that challenge Stick Candles were made in a garage in California, the basement of my parent's house, and a workshop in Upstate New York!

How long had you been in business before you decided to get premises and found The Old Forge? Was that always part of the plan?

I like to think that a lot of it is intentional and a lot of it is beyond my perception / conception of what's next. I am a surfer and I mention that for the analogy it provides. In surfing it has to be a combination of intent and conditions in equal parts, or at least in parts that will go together to create what really becomes magic!

If I had had a business-minded partner, a lot of our decisions would have resulted in lower overall value. We'd be more financially sound, for sure, but I doubt that we would have all of the elements that attract interest, sincere interest from our customers. From a business perspective it would have made more sense to make the candles in an inexpensive, perhaps less inspiring space. But of course that would lack the story that has become the core of our appeal. It's a hard argument to make, particularly to a bank or the government, especially in these times. But the value of magic cannot be assessed!

Words of wisdom. What's the best piece(s) of advice you've been given. What do you wish you'd known when you started out. Any advice for others thinking of doing their own thing?

The most helpful thing for me has been to listen to every person who shares an idea. You have to sift through a lot of things that you know from your own experience will not work, but the important things will come out of that.

When someone is willing to talk to you about what you are trying to do, you must listen.

Find a Mentor…find multiple mentors. Allow the conversation to take place.

Advice : Make mistakes. Do something. Do anything: until you succeed or fail.

What does the future hold for Stick Candles? Any exciting plans you'd like to share?

Candles are just the start. Once we have that running smoothly, I hope to be able to spend all of my time creating new objects for use and pleasure, whatever they are. I have notebooks full of great ideas. This is the first one to fall out of the notebook and take off. When I have taken the candles all the way, there will be many more ideas following right behind!!

Doug Collum's
Top Ten Tips for Creative Business Success

1) Do something : just thinking about your idea will keep it from "becoming".

2) Listen to any person who has the interest to talk to you about your idea.

3) Keep a Journal—even if you think your notes each day aren't valuable.

4) Make mistakes and examine them for what they tell you about the future.

5) Ask questions and see that a "No" is as valuable as a "Yes".

6) Examine challenges from every perspective.

7) Be transparent.

8) Make time for creative pleasure.

9) Re-examine successful developments.

10) Simplify.

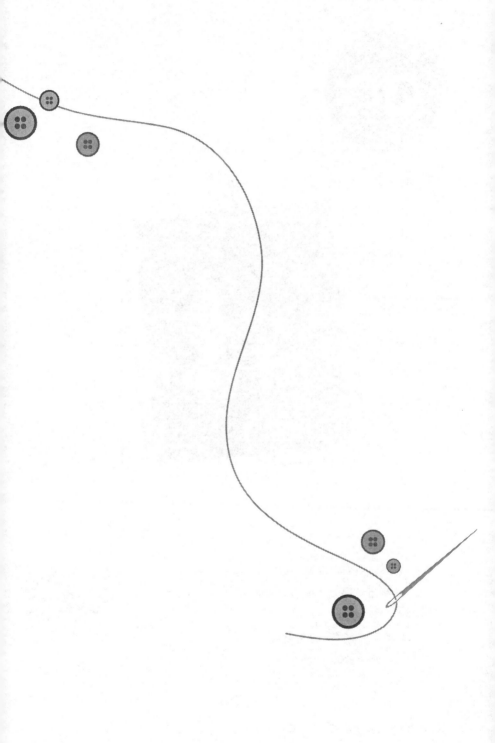

Name: **Abigail Percy and Ryan Bell**

Company Name: **abigail*ryan**

Location: **Belfast, Northern Ireland**

Website: **www.abigailryan.com**

abigail*ryan is the dream child of design duo, and couple, Abigail Percy and Ryan Bell. Working together, they combine Abigail's organic and nature inspired illustrations and Ryan's love and flair for color and graphic design to produce beautifully unique fabric and objects for the home.

All the home-wares produced under the banner of abigail*ryan are hand sewn in their Belfast fabric studio using 100% Pure Irish Linen.

Abigail Percy is an award winning jewelry designer born and raised in Glasgow, Scotland. She has run her own successful jewelry design company since 2005. Following her graduation from Glasgow School of Art with First Class honors, and winning The British Jewellers Association prize for 'One Year On', she has exhibited her work in venues such as the National Museum of Kyoto (Japan), The National Theatre (London) and the Scottish Gallery (Edinburgh) and has work in many private collections. In addition, Abigail undertakes private styling and business consultation for designers across the UK.

Ryan Bell hails from Northern Ireland and, since graduating from The University of Ulster at Belfast with a First Class honors degree in Fine Art Photography, he has worked on photography projects with various clients, including a division of Marks and Spencer, and worked with many individual designer makers across the UK— creating their brand identities through consultation and graphic design under the moniker "DesireLines".

In 2006, to feed Ryan's love of design and thirst for new challenges, and his desire to return to the more hands-on side of the creative industries, the DesireLines brand diversified into Luxury Accessories. Since then, the business has focused on creating stunning one off handbags and, since early 2009, several collections of Fine Silver Jewelry.

So you both have very established creative backgrounds—how did the idea for Abigail*Ryan homewares come about?

abigail*ryan homewares was born purely from our circumstances...we met each other through our Etsy shops, and began a long distance relationship, travelling between Belfast and Glasgow. While Ryan was staying with me in Glasgow, I taught him how to make jewelry in my home studio and we realized very quickly how much we loved working together! Creative ideas flowed as we sparked off each other, and we quickly decided we wanted to collaborate on something...we tossed around ideas for jewelry, for handbags, for almost anything, really—finally striking on the idea to turn my drawings into repeat pattern designs for fabric (at that stage, as possible handbag linings!)...the idea really developed from there—we were both keen lovers and consumers of lovely products for the home, so turning our printed fabric yardage in to cushions and such, and branching into tea-towels seemed like a good plan.

A simple, if not slightly depressing answer to this one—The Recession!

I went from having the busiest two years of my career, to one of the quietest, as the media flared with anti-spending hysteria! Whilst this could have spelled disaster, it all fell at the perfect time for us, as I was able to spend weeks at a time away from my workshop staying in Belfast with Ryan, where we worked on ideas and, when back home in the studio, I could attend to any orders that had trickled in, as well as having enough free time to focus on developing abigail*ryan homewares.

People say everything happens for a reason, and we think this is completely true —what could have been a very hard and depressing time, instead gave us both the time to re-assess what we wanted from our careers (when we normally would have been so neck deep in orders and work we couldn't have considered anything new or 'change') and it felt like an incredibly free, enjoyable and exciting time for us both!

There are tons of graphic designers and creatives out there who dream of using their designs on a range of products—but where to begin. It's such a competitive market. What research did you do and what made you decide to take the plunge?

We actually didn't do any research with regards to seeing who else was out there and making sure there was a gap in the market. We are, of course, aware of what is going on in design as consumers (who read design blogs and glossy home magazines regularly!)—but we didn't stop for a minute and think 'is there space for us'? Perhaps this could be seen as a little foolish, but I think we would both stand behind the principle of our thinking—if you are making something you are truly proud of, excited about, and think is market worthy, you shouldn't get bogged down in worrying about your competition...As long as you think you have (and do have, of course!) a unique point of difference, to make sure you set yourselves apart, it can be a very good thing to not concern (or worry!) yourself about what other people do. We did, however, do a good bit of research regarding what products we wanted to branch into—what type of value these items could yield and if it would be financially viable for us to make them.

You produce a range of textile products, all handmade in Northern Ireland using local linens. Do you do all the work yourself or employ any help with the printing/sewing etc?

We do a lot of the work ourselves. Currently, we outsource the printing of our tea-towels as we don't have enough space to screen print in our home studio, so that is a huge amount of work taken care of for us...we also have our yardage digitally printed, so it arrives with us ready to cut and sew!

We still cut, sew and finish all the cushions ourselves, from our home studio/kitchen table! This is a sizeable undertaking and is the biggest part of our 'making' work-load. We recently were faced with a very large order of cushions, and that forced us to look at the idea of outsourcing some of the work—we spent a lot of time researching local factories who might be able to undertake the work in their down-time. Finally we found someone who could do the work, so after lengthy discussions, we gave them all of our fabric, templates and instructions and crossed our fingers.

This was a big lesson for us—we are both control freaks in terms of quality and finish so we had to learn to let go! Unfortunately, things didn't work out... we received a call from the factory the morning they were supposed to deliver the order telling us it wasn't working... their industrial sewing machines were not able to do a part of the stitching we do on our domestic/professional machine and everything was getting chewed up. It was quite a shock for us—and we were left in the position of having to complete the order ourselves in the space of 24 hours, as they were due to be dispatched the following day!

Encouragingly, though, we managed it—and so, exhausting as it was, it forced us to realize our true manufacturing capabilities in terms of time and quantities possible.

With regards to expanding, we think we would look at piece work and/or hiring a skilled machinist to work for us, getting paid per item completed and keeping our very high quality control standards. With our experience of trying a factory now, we think it will be important to work with people who really care about what we do, what we create and our deadlines—working one to one with people would probably be the best way for us to achieve this, whether we bring someone in to the studio to work alongside us, or whether we create a remote, but more controlled, working relationship with individuals. Growing a business, and reallocating your time as you outsource can be a slow undertaking, but we feel confident we have plans in place to address every new challenge the business faces now.

Trade Fairs—An expensive, but necessary tool? Discuss.

We have actually just come back from our very first Trade Fair, so we don't have a lot of extensive experience to share! However, we do have a few thoughts with our first foray in to Fairs being a very positive one.

We have been lucky up until this year to be 'found' by many of our retail customers. For example, Terrain, part of the Anthropologie group, found us online and contacted us for our wholesale information, so you certainly can pick up suppliers without the expense of heading to a show. Even large and established stores will look at blogs and social networking sites to find new design talent!

We attended Pulse London this year, and were incredibly impressed with how the show was run. The team was smooth, professional, efficient and friendly in correspondence leading up to the show and that extended to the actual event itself. We won an award for 'Best New Launchpad Exhibitor Pulse 2011' so it was a very successful first outing for our homewares...we met lots of interesting people and received a few orders, too.

The general feedback from other more established designers we spoke to at the show is that attending Trade Fairs is a lot about putting your face 'out there' so you become part of the scene and are present in buyers/journalists consciousness. They don't necessarily pay off financially with orders during the show, or even follow up orders, instead we think you should maybe consider them part of your marketing budget as it's so much about creating brand awareness and making contacts for the future!

You have a great website for selling directly to the public. Do you also do any consumer fairs? Sell on Etsy or any other sites?

We have done some local Craft Fairs, with varying success. Christmas is a great time to attend fairs like this as people are always looking for stocking fillers and nice gift ideas.

We both had Etsy shops prior to starting abigail*ryan homewares (it's how we met!) and they can be very effective. A few downsides of selling through a site like Etsy is the fees you pay (although small, they do add up, especially if you are selling high-ticket items and, coupled with paypal fees, you can lose quite a bit of your item price), and that you are selling alongside an un-juried selection of goods with people who are not running a 'business'.

Now, while this, in itself, is not a problem, I found it a challenge when I sold my jewelry on Etsy as it has created a culture of a particular type of buyer. There are so many people on Etsy who do not price their products correctly, and professionally, and it can severely impact those who do. I know, for a fact, there are a lot of jewellers on Etsy who are barely covering the cost of their materials— giving the impression to some buyers that you are charging "too much". This, coupled with the anonymity of the Internet means that customers have been known to get in touch, and become quite aggressive—telling you that you are overpriced and that they will offer you X for an item, as if you are on an auction site. Etsy, and sites like it, have almost become a place like ebay, where people search for bargains... beautiful things for rock bottom prices. This makes for happy customers, but it can be hard to run a business in venues like these and price your goods for business purposes, such as also selling to Trade. Etsy, and other sites like it, seem to market to people who confuse handmade luxury with homemade bargains, and by staying un-juried, don't differentiate between those who want to create a high-end luxury item made by hand with the associated price-tag, and those working only to cover their material costs and for fun.

I like the website we use to run our shop from—there is a set monthly fee, and you can also remain autonomous. While Etsy has a fantastic community spirit, it has changed over the years and can now feel like wading through a lot of haystacks to find some 'needles'. Because the search engine works on how recently you have listed an item, the success of your shop can also rely all too easily on how much money you are willing to throw at your shop in re-listing fees, under the bracket of 'marketing'.

Having said all that, we recently set up an Etsy shop to allow people to purchase our goods priced in US Dollars. They have improved their system in the last few years, adding a currency converter so we don't have to keep on top of fluctuations —they do it for us!

BigCartel is an excellent template system for online shops, and we certainly recommend this as a great and easy to run option. There are many other similar options available, so it's well worth shopping around and finding the right fit for you.

We enjoy the mixture of selling directly to the public, and selling Wholesale. Wholesaling your goods can be very lucrative, and getting larger cash injections in to your business is a fantastic addition to your annual turn-over. While you lose at least 50% off the retail price, you also save time by bulk packaging and posting, so it certainly has it's advantages.

Please describe the space you work from? Has this changed from when you started out?

Our workspace is our home! When we moved in together over a year ago, we were combining our existing workshops as well as trying to create a permanent space for abigail*ryan homewares. Things didn't fit as well as we hoped they would, so the room we had earmarked for a workshop has become more of a storage/office space, as well as housing Abigail's jewelry bench.

We store all our materials (fabric yardage, rolls of linen, cushions, tea-towels, tools, paperwork) in the 'study' and now mainly work on the kitchen table for our manufacturing duties. Luckily, we have quite a lot of space, so have room for a small workstation in the kitchen—this keeps all the things we need to hand most often, and the items we are working on neat and tidy.

As we are rapidly expanding, though, our workspace will need to evolve, so we are currently saving up for a large log-cabin garden studio, which we will build at the end of our large garden...this will give us a dedicated work space for cutting/sewing, designing, drawing and such... it will be nice not to have to clear everything away for breakfast, lunch and dinner!

Words of wisdom! What sort of advice do you wish you had been given before you started out?

Our words of wisdom would mostly apply to the financial challenges you will face. For launching, sourcing a new product line and starting up—figure out how much money you will need and then double it! Things always cost more than you think they will, and things always go wrong...having a contingency fund is essential.

Regarding time, and how long you think a project will take—double that, too!

Especially when you are relying on other people to deliver goods, outsource services and such, you need to anticipate them not hitting the deadlines. You also need to factor in things such as holidays and getting ill. It's the curse of the self-employed...you will always get ill when you are run down and stressed, so if you give yourselves a little bit more of a time margin, things will feel easier.

These are all things we didn't do, so you could certainly learn from our past experience and mistakes!

Trust your instincts. So often, when things go wrong, or people let you down, you had a bad feeling about them at the start. It's very hard, especially when hindsight is 20/20, to advise you to trust your gut, but as our business goes on we are beginning to see a pattern emerge from challenges...they usually involve people/avenues we should have avoided in the first place!

Cash flow is a major challenge all businesses under 3–4 years of age will face. We wish we knew more about investors, funding opportunities and what other options were available to us.

And finally...what does the future hold for Abigail*Ryan? Any exciting plans you'd like to share?

We are just about to launch our Heirloom Collection, which comprises our one-off unique items ranging from throws, to quilts and floor cushions. Each one is lovingly hand made and intended to last a lifetime, especially the quilts and be handed down through generations. We are very excited to finish up some final pieces, photograph and style them, and design some special packaging for the items... lots of work still to do on this range, but it will be well worth it!

We will be attending Pulse London again next year, so will be working hard to develop new items and designs for our clients to see at Pulse.

We also had recent success at the Liberty of London's Best of British Open Call, so our cushions will shortly be appearing in the historic store. This is a dream come true for us both, as we so love and respect Liberty's approach and support of British designed and made goods. We feel so proud to have one of the most important stores in the UK, if not the world, endorse and support our designs!

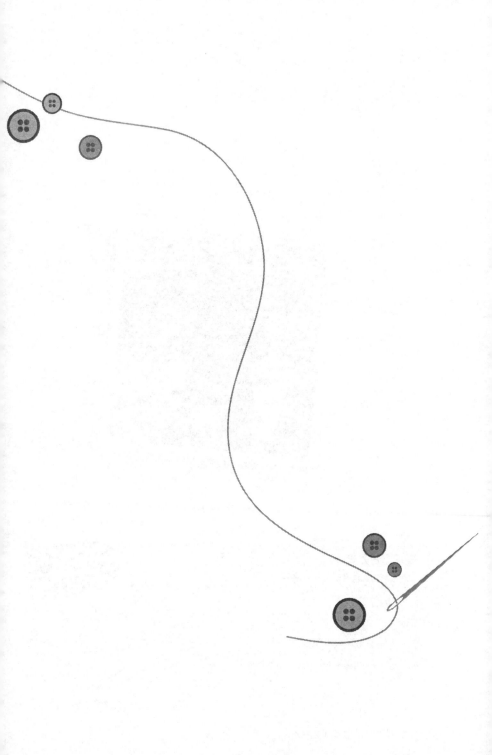

Poppy Treffry

Name: **Poppy Treffry**

Company Name: **Poppy Treffry**

Founded in: **2004**

Location: **Penzance, Cornwall, UK**

No. of Employees: **9**

Website: **www.poppytreffry.co.uk**

About Poppy Treffry: We are a small company and until very recently we were based in Newlyn—a busy, messy, industrious fishing village in the far west of Cornwall, England. In May of 2010 we moved to a much larger industrial unit in a quirky little business park in the woods just outside Penzance—so instead of fish we now have squirrels and woodpeckers!

Poppy started small, back in 2004, selling to one or two galleries locally, but many years on the team has grown from just Poppy and one cranky Singer sewing machine to 9 people and 13 cranky Singer sewing machines! The products are all still made in Cornwall and inspired by our beautiful surroundings and we plan to keep it that way! It's nice to feel we are providing a creative, friendly workplace in the county where we grew up.

Tell us a bit about yourself and what inspired you to start the business.

I did a textile design degree at Winchester School of Art and then volunteered with a craft cooperative in Guatemala, helping women to develop their business skills and supporting them in setting up a local craft shop. I'd only intended to stay a year but I got so involved in the project that I ended up staying for three! On my return to Cornwall in 2003 I began making bags with the idea of selling them, having taught myself freehand machine embroidery on an old Singer sewing machine that my granddad found on a dump! A business advisor saw the bags in the one gallery I dared to approach with them and helped me put together a business plan and to find a workshop and set up my own studio. At first I had a part time job as an Arts officer, but after 18 months I took the plunge to go full time and we've now been trading for about 8 years.

You started out sewing everything yourself on a vintage Singer sewing machine, and selling to a few local stores and galleries...at what point did you realize that it was time to employ some help?

It was quite early on that I realized I was going to need some help. The first person who got involved was my sister Faye in 2005, collecting a box of stitching to take home to do in the evenings when she was on maternity with her son! Faye gave up her proper job in 2006 and came to work for me full time, and she now manages all our marketing activities, the website and the shop in St Ives.

My next two girls, Briony and Freya approached me through friends and there was very little in the way of interviews—I needed help and fast so the only question was: can you learn fast and can you work fast?! I was very lucky and Briony now does the bulk of our embroidery and Freya puts together all the stitching boxes as well as an endless list of tasks that we try not to take for granted!

It is only recently that I have been able to hand over quite a bit of the people management and concentrate on product design and the direction the business is going in. So Sara has taken on the role of wholesale and production manager and she keeps the studio running and manages the studio assistants and outworkers and Faye manages the shop staff, web designer and pr. So in theory I will have more time for what I do best!

You now have your very own Poppy Treffry shop—how did that come about?

I must confess that I just really, really wanted a shop! I knew I wanted it in St Ives and I knew I wanted to tell the story of our 'brand' by putting all our products under one roof for people to see and understand. I did not do a massive amount of research beyond that. Of course I did spread sheets and predictions, got word of mouth advice on the area and costs, but the opportunity came along in the form of very affordable premises and I saw it as a chance to just dip my toe in at a fairly low risk level.

It has been a big learning curve but I'm really pleased we've done it—apart from anything else it has been a great advert for our business and people come to St.Ives just to find us. It's also really helped us understand how our customers respond to our products, and allowed us to monitor best sellers and wheedle out the products that don't go so well. But on the downside it is costly keeping it staffed and stocked, and St Ives is really seasonal and really weather dependent too so if the sun is shining everyone goes down to the beach and the shop is dead, and if it's been raining for 5 days straight people are too miserable to shop!

As well as all the textile items that you produce yourself, you now have a lovely new ceramics range. How did you find the right people to produce that?

I got a lot of advice from other designer makers on how to put the ceramics range together. I started out initially using a local company, but was not happy with the quality so then moved to Stoke where the current collection is made. I can't say it hasn't been without its ups and downs, and producing in England means that you are quite restricted on what you can develop as the costs are really high.

I am now very happy with the quality but there are still challenges; ordering and getting the stock levels right, storage, packing and sending, breakages and working with a ceramics industry that is always struggling to stay afloat makes your supply chain fragile and vulnerable to sudden changes. If I'm honest, I much prefer working with our textile products where I have more control and can do smaller runs of designs.

With such a wide range of products, that's a lot of stock! How do you store and distribute it all?

We have actually only just started keeping any stock for our wholesale orders. Historically we have always made everything to order, meaning a much longer turnaround for customers, but a much tighter ship for us in terms of stock. The main reason for the change was to streamline the production as we now work in monthly batches for production rather than weekly ones so everything is quicker and more efficient (she said confidently!)

Moving to the new premises has given us much more room to keep stock and we can now generally send out orders the day they come in rather than customers waiting 6–8 weeks. It is tricky managing the stock though and we are still learning about the best ways of doing this and gathering data to inform how we plan production going forward. We still have days when Freya is sewing emergency Christmas Egg cosies for an order to go out the same day as the stock control system didn't quite do its job!

Your products are stocked all over the world—how did you make the leap from supplying to UK shops to supplying internationally?

I have done the New York Gift Fair for the past two years and am due to go out again this January, and that is now building up a good stockists base in America. We try to be really quick in responding to their enquiries and have developed a wholesale website they can use and some of our marketing is aimed directly at the US market. Having said that, we have picked up Japanese and European stockists through the London tradeshows and through our press coverage, so you never know where they are going to come from!

We are still learning about how to manage the shipping, billing, customs and all that malarkey , and overseas trade is a lot more complicated than dealing with just the UK. We are planning on moving over to a new business management tool in the New Year which will ease a lot of these problems, and once you have put the procedures in place it is not too bad. I think the key is to maintain good communication—although we only have contact with our UK stockists through email and phone there is something about that geographical distance that can create quite a barrier to communication and you (or in our case Sara!) just have to manage that.

Trade Fairs—What was the first fair you showed at? Which shows do you still do?

Trade fairs have traditionally been the backbone of our business. I launched the company in 2004 at the British Craft Trade Fair in Harrogate along side 6 other Cornish makers, and my business moved to a whole other level in 2005 when I took part in the Top Drawer trade show in London for the first time. At both shows the amount of interest and orders in the book was staggering and quite difficult to manage production wise.

But as we've got more organized and more established, tradeshows are just one of the ways we bring in business. We have a lot of repeat custom and a wholesale website which works really well and we are definitely at a point now where we are much less dependent on them and next year we just plan to do one for the Christmas period, probably in London.

My worst tradeshow experience was probably the first time we did Pulse at Earls Court in London and we had a tiny stand right at the back and not even the organizers knew where it was! And on top of that they tagged an extra day on—

as if 3 days in dark aisle with tumbleweed blowing up it weren't enough! The best experience was probably Top Drawer in 2007 which was our best year to date. I just remember Faye and I ordering Champagne at the restaurant after we'd taken the stand down and giggling like loons! (Until we got home and thought—now we've got to make all this!)

Selling to retailers—how many stores are you now stocked in? How has this grown year on year. Was the growth slower or quicker than you had hoped for?

We are stocked in over 200 shops which was a far quicker growth than I ever anticipated. We are now working on actually reducing this down and honing it to 30 or 40 really good customers who completely buy in to the brand and can be ambassadors for what we are trying to achieve.

You have a great website for selling directly to the public. Do you also do any consumer craft or gift fairs? What % of your business is retail vs. wholesale?

Our website is the area of the business that we really want to grow as the return is better and we obviously have more control over how the brand is presented. That said, our business is approximately 70% wholesale and 30% retail so as one grows so does the other. We sell through notonthehighstreet.com and have done since they first launched, and we also sell at a couple of select retail shows including the Country Living Fair and the Contemporary Craft Fair in Bovey Tracey which are both great shows for us.

We see these other retail channels as a cost effective way of reinforcing our brand and getting our name out there as they have a much greater reach than us. Retail shows are also a great way of meeting the customers and getting genuine feedback on the products.

Cashflow—one of the biggest challenges of a small business owner. How have you financed the growth of your company?

The financial management of the company has always been my responsibility and at times it has been a real struggle. I am working with a book keeper for the first time this year which is really helpful and I have had a really good accountant right from the start. I have grown my business organically, investing the profits of one year in to growth for the next year. I'm naturally quite frugal—I think designer makers often are—and try to run a tight ship without taking too many financial risks. That said I have a very trusty gut feeling which on the whole does not let me down!

The business has grown a lot this year and I am delegating more of the staff management and purchasing, so it is proving harder to keep the finances tightly controlled, which is why we are planning to move over to more effective software for managing the business next year.

I have not had to go to the bank for loans and I didn't have an overdraft until 2010, but can see that it is a useful tool as the orders and the bills get bigger and the payment terms longer! I had always enjoyed the financial management aspect of the business and felt quite proud that I do all the payroll myself as it's another string to my bow, but as the company has grown this has become more and more complicated—and I've also had a baby and no matter what anyone says there are certain brain cells that you never get back!

You also have a baby daughter. How do you manage to balance running a business with being a parent?

I won't lie, juggling my daughter and the business can be a real struggle! I'm lucky in that she is a really easy child and has fitted in around my work since day one really. I think I have a (perhaps unhealthy) obsession with my work, so taking a back seat and scaling things back was never really an option! Biba just fits in. For the first 6 months she came to work and had a cot, toys etc there and now she has a combination of nursery, grandmas and dad as he and I share the parenting 50/50. I think if he were not so supportive and so involved then it would have been a very different story. She still comes to work quite a bit and I've already bought her, her first tiny vintage sewing machine for Christmas! It would be lovely to think that one day she'll work in the business too.

Poppy Treffry's
Top Ten Tips for Creative Business Success

1) Get your pricing right.

2) Make your product original by looking in unusual places for inspiration.

3) Yours business is YOU, so don't try to be something you're not.

4) Get as much help and support as you can, especially from people with a critical eye.

5) Get a website—even if it's small at first.

6) Invest in good photography—go in with other designers to share the cost.

7) Make full use of free online tools and information portals.

8) Get out and about, networking and talking to people about your idea.

9) Set your sights high and chose a few businesses to follow and be inspired by —even though might sell something totally different.

10) Put down some core values, and don't be afraid to make enjoying what you do part of this!

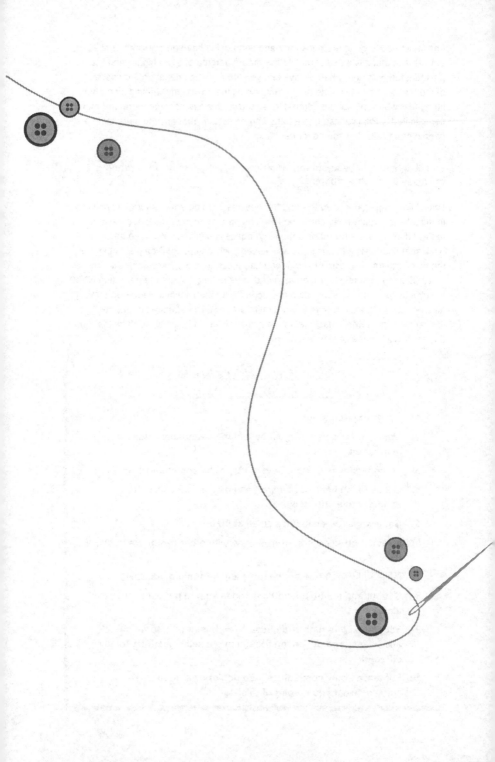

oliver + s

Name: **Liesl Gibson**

Company Name: **Liesl + Co. (Oliver + S and Lisette sewing patterns)**

Founded in: **2007**

Location: **Brooklyn, NYC, USA**

No. of Employees: **4 staff and several freelancers**

Website: **www.oliverands.com / www.sewlisette.com**

After earning a degree in fashion design from the Fashion Institute of Technology (FIT) in NYC, Liesl Gibson worked as a designer for several top fashion brands, including Tommy Hilfiger and Ralph Lauren.

In 2008 Liesl + Co. launched its first brand, Oliver + S, which produces patterns, fabrics, and other products for sewing children's clothing. Oliver + S products are available on the company's website and through independent fabric stores worldwide. Liesl + Co. launched the Lisette brand of patterns and fabric in the spring of 2011, and Liesl's first book, *Oliver + S Little Things to Sew*, which features 20 full-length projects for children's accessories, was published by STC Craft-Melanie Falick Books in 2011.

In 2010 she was given the FabShop Network's Rising Star Award, an honor bestowed by independent fabric store owners across North America.

Tell us how the idea for Oliver + S came about?

You know, I never intended to start a company that produced sewing patterns. But here's where I am today.

Before my daughter was born, I was a fashion designer in New York. After I had her, it just wasn't feasible for me to go back to work full-time. My husband was traveling four days a week for his job, and I did really want to spend more time with my daughter.

So, to keep entertained, I gave myself the challenge of designing and sewing a new wardrobe for my daughter each season. I began by looking at the children's sewing patterns that were available in the market, and nothing inspired me to sew. So, since I had the pattern making skills, I started to make my own designs for her. I had just started a blog, and I began posting photos of what I made for her. People began asking me if they could buy the patterns, and I would occasionally get stopped by someone on the street who asked where I got my daughter's clothes.

A friend encouraged me to make my patterns available for sale. My husband helped me write a business plan. And after a long time spent doing market research and product development, I launched Oliver + S with four pattern styles for little girls.

Did you continue to work while you launched the business?

I think it took well over a year from when I first started writing the business plan until we had product available. I was my daughter's primary caregiver during this time, and I was working on the company with all the free time I had. I put in a lot of very late nights during that year and was exhausted much of the time.

In the early days, I worked on the business myself, but I had input and assistance from several people. My husband was a management consultant at the time, and he helped with the business plan. Brooke Reynolds created our brand identity, packaging, website design, and first trade show booth. She was instrumental in creating the distinctive style that Oliver + S has. Once we launched and had product to sell, I hired a part-time assistant to help with filling orders and other office-related tasks. It wasn't until we had grown quite a bit that my husband left his job and joined me in the business as the first full-time employee beside me.

Describe the space you work from now? How does this compare to when your first started?

We have studio and office space now in an old, converted industrial building in Brooklyn. Our whole floor of the building used to be a book bindery, and we have old sewing needles embedded into the cracks in the floor between the wood floor boards. I've always thought this is a nice touch for our sewing space!

When I started Oliver + S, I was working from our small apartment in Manhattan. But we quickly determined that I needed a dedicated workspace. When I was working, I would cover all available surfaces in our small apartment with my pattern making paper and tools, and there was no room for anyone else. So taking a commercial space became an imperative pretty quickly for us. If we lived in the suburbs and had a large house with an extra bedroom or two, I wouldn't have had to take a commercial work space as quickly as I did.

Your business has now grown considerably and you have some great staff on board. At what point did you know you needed help?

There are two main reasons to add staff to a small growing business, and we've added staff for both of them. Either you have so much work you need to do that you can't do it all and you find you need assistance. Or you find the right person and you decide that bringing that person on board will allow you to take on new challenges and grow the business beyond where it is at present.

Your online store is beautiful and has various functions beyond just selling patterns. How important is it to invest in a good website?

I've been fortunate to have a business partner who is good at technology, which is very important for our business. He was instrumental in getting our website set up and growing it slowly over time to have more functionality. We've found that it's very important to have a website that is about more than just selling product. Our website is our most cost effective way of marketing our business, so we've invested in features there that will get people to engage with the brand and keep returning.

The growth trajectory for the Oliver + S brand has been slow and steady. Most of our wholesale customers are long-term customers, and we grow by having new stores pick up the line. We sell the Oliver + S products solely into the independent fabric store market, and that industry has one major trade show that occurs twice a year, International Quilt Market. We exhibit at this show. That was where we got our first exposure to the wholesale customer base, and we continue to show there to keep the market aware of our newest products. Most distributors from countries outside the US attend this show, and that's how we've established relationships with our distributors around the world.

Trade shows are a lot of work and are quite expensive to do. I'm always exhausted and physically sore when a show is done. There's nothing glamorous about exhibiting at a trade show, believe me. We get approached about exhibiting at other trade shows quite often, but we've never been convinced that the benefits of doing them will offset the costs.

For us, the reason we did the book was to expand the range of Oliver + S products in the market and to introduce new customers to the brand. If you are going to take the enormous amount of time it takes to do a book, you need to be sure that you have a reason for doing it. Unless you somehow manage to write the best-selling book of the year in the craft category, you'll end up making less than minimum wage on an hourly basis considering the amount of time you put into writing and marketing the book. Craft books just aren't money making ventures!

I had some insight into how to sell a book proposal because I began my career as a book editor, believe it or not. (After that I spent a few years doing equity research on Wall Street before I returned to school to earn a degree in fashion design.) And I was also fortunate to have some friends who had published craft books and were willing to coach me on what was expected in a craft book proposal.

When I was ready to shop the book around, I put together a pitch book for the concept which included information about the Oliver + S brand, a proposed table of contents, some sample project materials, and a biography of me. I made a list of the publishing houses that I could see taking the book and got in touch with the craft editors there. There were several publishers that bid on the book, and we then had a hard decision to make about which offer to accept. For us, because this was intended to be a brand-building project, being able to publish a book that "felt" like Oliver + S was even more important to us than the royalty rate and the advance offered. We eventually went with the publisher that we thought would be the best fit. And we've been very happy with how the book turned out.

You're now also and award-winning fabric designer and on your 3rd collection for Moda. Congratulations! How did this come about?

Well, I've won an industry award, and I've designed fabric collections, but I wouldn't consider myself an award-winning fabric designer!

Finding a manufacturer to license a fabric collection is much the same as finding a publisher to publish a book. When I decided it was time to produce an Oliver + S line of fabric, I put together concepts for the first collection I wanted to do. I then made a list of the manufacturers who I thought would be interested in the line, and I arranged meetings with their design directors.

Again, deciding on whom to work with came down to more than just the money. We ultimately made the decision to work with Moda for the fabric line because of how that relationship would help the Oliver + S brand overall.

In 2011, while Oliver + S was still growing, you launched a completely new brand called Lisette. Why did you decide to do that?

I had always wanted to do a women's apparel sewing line, but I faced a problem. There are two different distribution channels for sewing products—independent stores and chain stores. We designed Oliver + S to be sold only through independent stores. The problem is that the majority of apparel sewing in the US is done with products purchased at chain stores. Independent stores, for the most part, are quilting stores that carry printed cotton. (All the Oliver + S patterns are designed to be sewn with printed cottons, so they can be sold by quilt stores that carry only that kind of fabric.) But I wanted to do a line of sewing patterns and fabrics that would include apparel fabrics like lawn, canvas, twill, corduroy, etc. Most independent stores don't carry these kinds of fabrics, so the line I envisioned wasn't possible to produce for the same market as Oliver + S sells in.

I knew we needed to work with the chain stores to bring this line to market, since they are the only stores that carry these apparel fabrics. But I also knew that the chain stores are not interested in working with small companies like ours. From their perspective there's too much risk working with small companies, and they don't want to have business relationships with thousands of little companies. So I knew we needed to find partners for this brand.

We pitched the idea for this new brand to a contact we had at Fabric Traditions, which is a major fabric supplier to chain stores. She liked the idea and was interested in producing the fabric. She provided an introduction to the team at Simplicity which has a strong presence on the sewing pattern side with the chains, and we presented the idea to them. They were interested as well. So we approached Jo-Ann stores here in the United States first because they are the largest chain. They were excited by the concept, so we developed the line primarily for them—at first. Now you can also purchase Lisette products at other places as well. The Lisette fabrics are now available at the Spotlight chain in Australia, and Lisette patterns are available anywhere worldwide that Simplicity patterns are sold.

We couldn't have developed and launched this brand without our business partners, and they provide a lot of support in producing the pattern and fabric line.

You've been lucky enough to gain tons of press coverage. Did/do you do your own PR?

When I first launched the company, I hired a PR consultant who works in the fabric industry to help get word out about the company. Results on that effort were mixed. It cost a lot, and at the end of the day the coverage that resulted probably wasn't worth the investment.

Since then, we've done all our own PR in-house. We'll provide samples of new product each season to select fabric manufacturers, magazine and website publishers, and bloggers. But it's not magazine coverage that sells patterns these days. It's people writing about their experience sewing with a pattern on their blogs. We can tell the moment a prominent blogger posts something about one of our patterns because we start getting an unusual volume of website orders flowing in for one item.

To get people to want to blog about your product, you have to have a great product that people love and enjoy using. These testimonials are the best form of endorsement a product can get, and they really do encourage other people to buy the item too.

You blog, and both Oliver + S and Lisette have great online presences. Flickr groups, Facebook, Twitter – How do you find the time?!

There's never enough hours in the day. We would really like to do much more with the blogs on both the Oliver + S and Lisette sites, but if we did it would take time away from developing new product which is, after all, what pays the bills. But keeping your brand in front of your customers with good blog content, interesting Tweets, useful Facebook wall posts, etc. is just good business. So we make the time to do this, but we wish we could do even more.

I really do enjoy this aspect of running a business. One of my greatest pleasures is looking through the photos that get posted in our Oliver + S Flickr group and seeing so many happy children wearing our styles. I love it that I can help people create unique, one-of-a-kind items for their children and grandchildren and I love to see the results of what our customers do with my patterns.

Liesl Gibson's
Top Ten Tips for Creative Business Success

1) Develop a solid business plan before starting your business.

2) Manage your business to that plan.

3) Produce the best, highest quality product that you can.

4) Find the time to feed your creative spirit while running your company.

5) Provide excellent customer service.

6) Be reliable; deliver what you promise when you promised to deliver it.

7) Hire experts (a lawyer, accountant, web developer, customer service professional, etc.) to help you out in areas where you don't have expertise or interest.

8) Never believe your own press; you're only as good as the next product you create.

9) Market yourself and your business effectively; don't be a wallflower, but don't be bold and brash either.

10) Always look for partnership opportunities that will provide you and your prospective partner with a win-win.

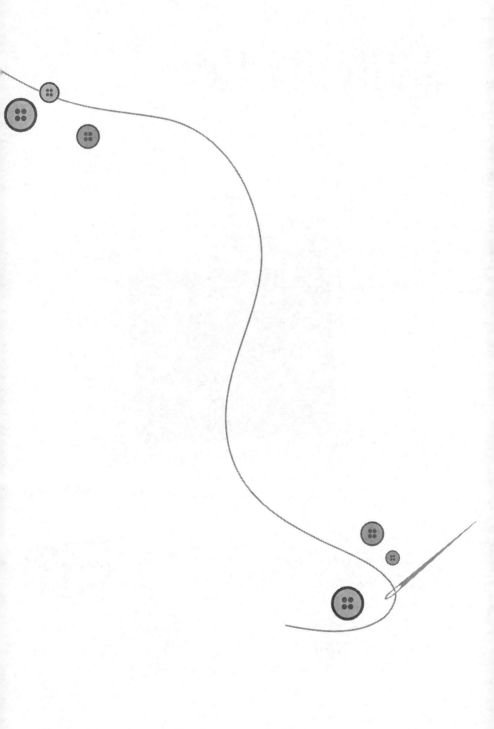

Stitchtastic

Name: **Sarah and Patrick Scott**

Company Name: **Stitchtastic**

Founded in: **2007**

Location: **Sheffield, UK**

Website: **www.stitchtastic.com**

My career background is as a science teacher, which really has very little to do with cross stitch! Stitchtastic came about through Patrick's mum initially. She taught me to cross stitch (although she admits now that she didn't think I'd take to it!) and I enjoyed myself stitching for a few years until I started to feel that were very few designs out there I actually wanted to stitch. So Patrick and I decided to start up our own company producing cross stitch charts and kits. We started with some motorbike and car designs and quickly moved on to caricatures along the transport theme, which was when we got our first licence deal to produce them from the original artwork. Since then, we've been building up the range and, more recently, we've started to bring other artists on board, including Anne Edwards, Kate Mawdsley and our very own Patrick, who is busy designing his own range as we speak! Patrick's background is in IT, so he was ideally placed to create our online presence and work on the online marketing side of things.

Cars, bikes, campervans, airplanes and vehicles! Your kits are pretty unusual for the traditional world of cross-stitching. How did you know there would be a market for these kinds of designs? Did you do lots of research?

Erm.....not really! We spoke to another designer who had produced some similar designs before us but had left the market quite recently due to time constraints. We also looked around online and ordered a few other designers' catalogues to see what was around, so we knew the sorts of designs that did exist that were perhaps slightly different to 'the norm'. Then we started off selling through e-bay, to get a feel for how popular the designs could be before creating our own website. The caricature work was very popular as artwork already, so we knew that when we negotiated the licence.

I suppose the best thing I can say is that I knew what I would stitch, and we took things slowly and got rid of anything that didn't prove popular. In this industry, you have to create a fine balance between pushing your designs for a while to ensure that they do get out there and get the publicity they deserve, and also not wasting money on creating and promoting things that simply don't sell.

Describe the space you work from?

We both work from home, but we work on different floors so we do have individual space. I work from the dining room which is actually half dining room, half office and Patrick works from his office upstairs. He worked from home before we started the cross stitch business, so he's quite used to the environment and I have always enjoyed working at home when I was teaching, so I don't find it difficult to switch from work to home mode. When I tell people we work from home, we are often asked 'How do you settle down to work? I'd be distracted all of the time'. I tend to answer that by explaining that if I'm distracted, I won't earn any money!

I have lots of cross stitch on the walls at home to inspire me, either stitched by me or Patrick's mum. My favorite and most inspirational piece is a sampler stitched by my great grandma and was passed onto me last year when a relative died. I had no idea it existed until I received it, and as you can imagine I was absolutely thrilled. It's dated 1899 and I shall keep it forever!

Patrick is inspired by the 2000 cones of thread he has on shelves around his room! We keep our stock of kits in the garage which has been waterproofed, sealed and fitted with shelving. We pride ourselves on sending out products quickly, so we do keep a fair amount of kit stock, but charts are printed out as they are ordered.

Do you produce all of your kits yourself? How did you source all the components and find the right parts?

We do produce all of our kits in-house. Because we have quite a big range, we tend to produce and sell small numbers of each different design so outsourcing would be too expensive for small runs. Having said that, we would certainly consider it if one or two designs became extremely popular or we received a very large trade order.

Finding the right parts all came down to my own personal stitching preferences. I like to stitch with DMC threads on Zweigart aida, so that's what we include in our kits. We tend to make the kits in sets of 20, which isn't too bad for storage, and at the present time we don't employ any other staff. Our busiest time is after the Craft Hobby and Stitch International Trade Show in February. We spend a lot of time afterwards preparing the orders we have taken there. Most retailers are happy to wait a couple of weeks for products, so there's never been a problem with that. Also, quality control is easier when produced in-house, plus outsourcing can entail long lead and delivery times. So if at all possible, we shall continue to produce in-house, until the time comes that 24 hour a day working is not enough!

How did you work out what prices to retail your kits at? Is there a formula that you use?

Pricing is always difficult. We did our research here and looked around a great deal at other producers of cross stitch. We didn't want to price ourselves out of the market, but also we needed to cover our costs and make a little bit too so that we could eat! Patrick is in charge of the costings and he's very good at including all of the costs, those of the raw materials and the labour (even though it's us, we do need to include an element of labour cost). The usual formula for selling to trade is that shops will take your wholesale price and multiply it by 2.4 (double plus VAT) to calculate their retail price.

Initially we were only selling retail and the pricing worked for us, but when it came to selling to trade we realized if we used the 2.4 multiple our trade price would be far too low, which meant raising our RRP before we could start selling wholesale. So for anyone working out their pricing I would say to not only consider the raw material costs and your profits but also whether you might want to sell to trade in the future.

Of course, over the last few years pricing has become even more difficult with the massive price rises in cotton. Our suppliers charge us more for raw materials and we get squeezed in the middle. Very frustrating!

Thanks, I'll pass that on to Patrick! He designed our store from scratch. There are plenty of software packages that will produce a store for you and manage sales, and we did use one initially while we were still finding our feet, but we find that a personally designed site works better for us as Patrick can design exactly what we want and how we want it to look. Obviously, not all businesses are lucky enough to have a Patrick, so we do appreciate that software packages are fantastic for most people.

When we first started selling online, I was so excited! I can remember receiving our first order and not having a clue what to do next. However, we now have a management system that produces invoices for us at the click of a button and we can easily access order details securely online, so we can check orders even when we're not at our desks.

After we'd been selling for a little while, we realized that a lot of cross stitchers didn't have access to the internet, although I'd say that has decreased since we started out. So we produced a paper catalogue and offered it free as part of our advertising campaigns in the cross stitch magazines. We had a really good take up and so now we take orders by post and on the phone as well—we're on our third catalogue right now. Again, I can vividly remember my first phone order where I had to take a credit card payment. I was so scared I might do it wrong and charge someone £3200 rather than £32.00!

Stock management is all done on computer as well. We have our kits in certain areas of the shelving system and the computer can tell us where they are and how many are left. It sounds complicated but it isn't when you know how!

We have always found shipping hard work and expensive. We use Royal Mail for the majority of our deliveries and the lady in our local post office knows us very well. Last year we invested in a franking machine to reduce postage costs, but I would certainly advise people to wait a while before thinking about franking. It's an expensive outlay, contracts can be quite long, and you need to know how much postage you're likely to use in a year before you get into complicated negotiations with franking companies. For larger parcels, we use a number of companies, mostly through Parcel to Go (www.parcel2go.com) who provide access to a number of different delivery services. We also keep a proof of postage for everything we send, in case of loss by the postal service. Luckily, we've had very few of these. We've had incredibly few returns or complaints in our time, I'm happy to say. We abide by distance selling regulations and so if a customer returns their product, we give them a refund. I could count on one hand the number of complaints we've had in 4 years and long may this continue! All I can say is that the customer is (unfortunately!) always right and you have to deal with complaints politely, fairly and with a positive attitude.

We did some retail fairs when we first started and this kind of prepared us for the trade fairs. At present, we do just the 1 trade fair per year—Craft, Hobby and Stitch International in February—and we do get a lot of publicity from that which leads to a large number of trade orders through the year, in addition to those placed at the show itself, so it is well worth doing. Our first trade show was in 2009, so we'd been trading for a good 2 years direct to customers before we ventured into trade. We do find the show useful and may consider adding another one to the calendar, but they are incredibly hard work and murder on the feet! Our designs attract people to our stand, but it is sometimes tricky to persuade retailers that our designs are very popular and do sell, particularly if they have a very traditional clientele. Having said that, when they do place an order they do come back for more!

You sell directly to the public via your website AND wholesale to lots of shops and online stores. What % of your business would you say is wholesale vs retail.

I would say that over 50% of our sales are retail, but I wouldn't like to go any further than that as things do change quite frequently. The big advantage of selling to shops is that they can deal with the marketing. They often have a very loyal client base who will try designs if they stock them, which gets our name out there to a whole area of stitchers who may not otherwise get to hear of us.

We have a large base of other online retailers who also sell our products. Patrick provides them with a data feed of all of our products and they e-mail or phone us when an order is placed, and we then post out to them within a couple of days and they can then post out to the customer. They're great as they are often very high up in the search engines for quite general terms such as 'cross stitch', whereas we are high up for more specific terms such as 'car cross stitch' or 'caricature cross stitch'. We also sell on Amazon, which we fulfil ourselves.

Marketing, databases etc. Do you have a core of regular customers? How do you keep in touch with them and generate new sales from existing customers etc?

I think this is the hardest part of the business actually and is a never ending process. We do have a core of regular customers, we have our facebook fans (www.facebook.com/Stitchtastic, click on Like!) and we send out a newsletter to several thousand customers every month that I write. Magazine marketing is also very important in the craft industry. We've spent a long time building up relationships with the magazines, both retail and trade and we advertise every month in at least 2 trade and 2 retail magazines, which admittedly costs a fortune but is worth it. Free editorial is the holy grail, but it is incredibly difficult to get on a regular basis and may well involve a giveaway of products or a competition.

My advice on using marketing to generate new sales, for what it's worth, would be to keep trying and to never give up, even when you think you'll never be featured anywhere!

How have you financed the growth of your company—did you have to approach the banks for loans?

When we started the business I was still teaching full time and continued to do so until 2008, when I went part time and eventually left altogether, although I do still occasionally fill in at schools I like! So this helped us initially. We were able to start out selling just charts which were stored on computer and printed when ordered, so this reduced costs although we did have to invest in really good quality color and black and white printers. So we're very lucky that we haven't had to take out any loans. As the sales of charts increased, we used that money to finance buying a few DMC cones to start making a few kits and things just built up from there. We've not had any real problems with payment from retailers, and on the very rare occasion we have, a gentle reminder via e-mail or phone usually does the trick. We usually take payment before sending out products, although some of our larger trade customers pay after 30 days. However most prefer to leave their credit card details stored securely with us so that we can take payment whenever they order and they don't have to worry about it.

As a couple running a business together, how do you switch off and spend quality time together?

As I said earlier, we work on separate floors so we don't get in each other's way, which I think is very important. We make sure we have other things going on in our lives (such as my hobby as chair of the local amateur dramatics group) so that we do have other things to talk about. But we do talk about the business quite a lot and I don't really see anything wrong in that, it's a very important part of our lives. Plus we have a lot of friends who we (OK, I) can gossip with who are not really interested in cross stitching at all! Switching off is not as hard as people think. I can compartmentalise the house so that when I'm in the lounge I know I'm not working and when I'm in the office I am. It's just a case of putting your mind to it. Plus, working from home means we can plan to spend a lot more quality time together then most people. We can plan in days off during the week instead of at the weekend when everywhere is busy!

Any advice for those starting out?

When we started out, I wish I'd known that marketing and publicity is more important than anything else. I wish I'd been on a marketing course and I'd built up relationships with magazines earlier on but hey, *je ne regrette rien*...For others thinking of starting up, if you can, make sure you have another source of income for at least the first couple of years. Don't bank on a craft business as an escape from a terrible job, as it may well never reach that point and if it does, in the meantime you'll hate your job even more as you'll be doing that as well as your new business. Some craft businesses stay as hobby businesses forever and just bring in pocket money, and if that suits you, there's nothing wrong with that.

And finally...what does the future hold for Stitchtastic...any exciting plans you'd like to share?

Well, we're moving in a new direction with our designs and doing something we've always wanted to do ever since we started the business. We're showcasing the work of artists and this year we have 2 artists on board, Kate Mawdsley and Anne Edwards. We're particularly excited about this as the designs are animal based and I love them! Also of course, we're very excited about Patrick's range of designs. He has been thinking about designing for a couple of years now and is currently producing a range of very different designs which appeal to him and, we hope, to lots of other stitchers!

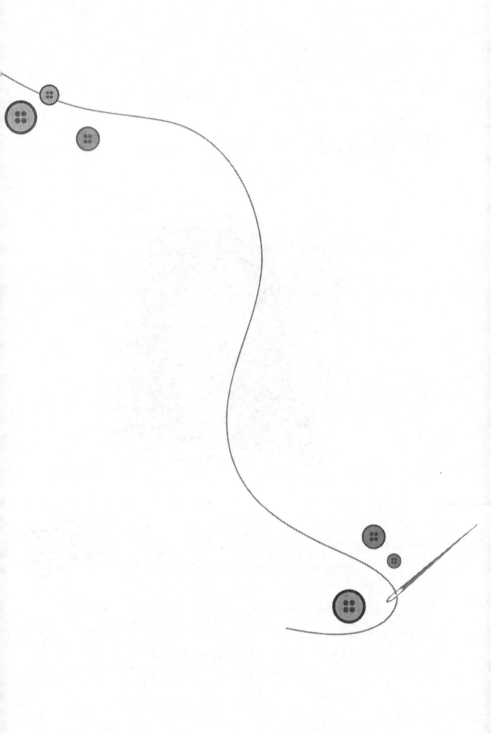

Name: **Jenny Hart**

Company Name: **Sublime Stitching**

Founded in: **2007**

Location: **Austin, Texas 2001–2010 / Los Angeles, California 2010–forever!**

No. of Employees: **2**

Website: **www.sublimestitching.com / www.jennyhart.net**

Sublime Stitching was founded independently in Austin, Texas in 2001 by Jenny Hart, due to an overabundance of bunny-n-duckie patterns and outdated, overly-difficult instructions for embroidery. After first trying embroidery in the summer of 2000, Hart was unable to find any alternative patterns for stitching ("alternative" meaning: anything other than cutesy teddy bears, duckies, bunnies and scarecrows). Instead of waiting for the craft industry to do something new, she did it herself. Jenny decided to create the company she wished existed: introducing her own designs in non-traditional themes, with new education and new anything for embroidery.

Sublime Stitching introduced edgy embroidery design, all-in-one embroidery starter kits and entertaining, now-I-understand-it instructions to bring embroidery back to life for a new generation of needleworkers. Hart's pioneering take on an ages-old handcraft was met with worldwide press, and hordes of loyal crafters, thankful for finally having the first alternative to geese in bonnets. (Things got a little crazy after that.)

Hart's vision for updated embroidery has grown from her first line of four design sheets to over fifty themes, including the collaborative Artist Series, and a complete product line that includes quality tools and textiles for embroidery. Through Sublime Stitching, Jenny has taught embroidery to thousands with her uniquely clear instructions, books, workshops and appearances. The tremendous success of Hart's signature embroidery style led to a series of titles of the same name with Chronicle Books.

Hart's hand-embroidered portraits are included in many private and public collections that include Carrie Fisher, comedian Tracey Ullman and Elizabeth Taylor.

Before launching Sublime Stitching, Hart first received international attention for her fine art and portraits in embroidery which have been exhibited and published throughout Europe, South America, Mexico, and Japan. Her work has been featured in publications that include SPIN, Real Simple, Rolling Stone, Vogue (Italy) BUST, ReadyMade, The New York Times, Entrepreneur, The Wall Street Journal and many others, and her work is included in the permanent collection of the Smithsonian American Art Museum.

Prior to starting Sublime Stitching you were a successful textile artist— did you always plan to start a business?

Well, I can't really say I am a textile artist. I am an artist who began experimenting with embroidery. I have no background in sewing, textiles or fiber art, which is what I think of when I hear "textile artist". It was not my area of specialty at all and I work in several different media—but embroidery became a newfound obsession.

I also can't say I had always planned to start a business, but after I began embroidering on my own, and the response to my work was so overwhelming, I decided for sure that I wanted to create a new design company for embroidery. I decided to make the embroidery company I wished existed when I was trying to learn how to do it. So, I designed new patterns you couldn't get, the tools that I liked and used the most, and started pre-assembling starter kits and bringing it all together the same way it came together for me. I really want to inspire as many as people as possible to give hand-embroidery a try.

Sublime Stitching was started on a loan of $1,000 from my dad. All money that I made I put back into the company. No big bank loans, just being as resourceful and as careful as possible.

Do you produce all of your kits yourself? When you started out, how did you source all the right components? Would you ever outsource your kit production to a big company?

Yes, I design and manufacture all of my kits. I used to personally assemble each kit myself, but that's no longer possible! I now have a helper who puts them together in-house.

Sourcing is research, and it can take days to years to find what (and who) you are looking for depending on what, and how unique it is. What I offer today has changed many times over the years to work out kinks and make improvements, so it's an ongoing process. There's no simple answer to sourcing except that it requires patience, persistence, trial and error and finding what you are looking for. And, that can take years. I work with a traditional print shop to make my patterns. However, they warehouse and manufacture proprietary materials that I have provided them to make my patterns. What they do for me, I specifically laid out and developed. It's like going to a seamstress: they do sewing, but they won't design the dress or pick the fabric for you. They do the work you hire and direct them to do with the materials you supply.

When I was doing all the kits by hand myself, an order of 20 kits seemed massive. Now, we have to be able to handle an order of 100 kits or more. Getting larger orders is the impetus for growth, because it forces you to make decisions about how you need to make changes in order to take on that increased business (if you want to). For me, it's crucial that my supplies be of really high quality. Scaling up to make more product often means turning to faster, cheaper and lower quality. But, I work very hard to be able to scale up and maintain the quality of my product.

"Outsourcing to a big company" isn't something that you can just do like a snap of your fingers. Who is this "big company"? Do they already make what you want to offer? Do they just do one little part of it? Are they strictly manufacturers or do they also retail themselves what they make? Are you licensing to them, or hiring them as a contractor? If they are a large manufacturer, the chances are they won't be interested in manufacturing for you unless you are producing in very high numbers. And, it's extremely difficult to find the right company who can make your product the way you want them to. None of these are easy and there are no simple answers. It's an ocean of information and possibilities.

I knew I had to hire help when I could no longer do it all by myself. The breaking point is when you realize that trying to do it all yourself is actually hurting your business rather than helping it. It's very tough to do, and finding the right people to take over what you were doing yourself is a brand new challenge. I couldn't really afford it, but I knew that I couldn't afford not to hire someone. I knew that if I did hire help, that would allow me to focus my energies on other work, the work that only I can do within the business to help it grow. You're kind of always taking the next step before you're completely ready for it, because at the same time you know taking that difficult step will eventually make it easier. That's what "growing pains" and leaps of faith are all about.

What have been your experiences of doing craft fairs and Trade shows?

The first fair I showed at was the first Renegade Craft Fair in Chicago in 2003. I continued to do every Renegade in Chicago until 2007. I've also done ICE (Indie Craft Experience), UCU (Urban Craft Uprising), Bazaar Bizarre, Maker Faires, and some others I'm probably forgetting!

The first professional trade show where I exhibited at was TNNA in 2004 and I have also shown (not by myself, however) at CHA and attended the Houston Quilt market. These are large, to-the-trade only shows, and they are expensive to participate in. A booth can cost at a minimum $700. I did it for 3-4 years and found that I benefited more from attending these events rather than exhibiting at them.

While some of my wholesale accounts came as a result of showing at professional trade shows, I really think the majority came about from seeing my website. Also, any time I'm in a store (as a customer, usually checking out local shops when I'm traveling) that I really like and think my stuff would fit in well with, I ask if the manager or buyer is in and just say "I love your store, you / he / she might be interested in what I do" and I leave a promo card.

The indie craft shows that have been flourishing for the last ten years can be truly wonderful experiences. They are much more personal and fun. The first few Renegade Craft Fairs felt like a big indie-internet-DIY reunion. Nearly everyone there knew one another from connecting online for the last couple of years and now we were all convening to meet! It was really, really exciting and fun. It still is. I did the Los Angeles Renegade Craft Fair this past summer and shared a booth with seamstress Christine Haynes. My mom came and helped out. It was great!

The hard part about doing small markets is people who come to your booth sometimes feel it's okay to grill you about how you make your product or what your sources are. It's really bad etiquette because, like I said before—what you do is the result of a lot of hard work and time and effort. You're there to sell or show off the results of your hard work. And, you're tired from setting up, stressed about taking orders, and trying to have a good time. So, it can be very awkward and uncomfortable when you are asked, because not everyone understands that they're asking you questions that don't just have simple answers. Would you go into a restaurant and ask the chef to come out and give you his recipes?

The hard part about large trade shows I've found is that they cater very, very strongly to large, established businesses. This means, they have the best positioning on the trade show floor and are grandfathered in for the best exposure. It feels to me more like business convention with exhibitors asking each other why their customers are disappearing and organizers saying they really wish they could attract more, younger designers to enliven the show—but they don't change how the organization is run.

> You're an author too! Most creative crafters would dream of securing a book deal—how did you get yours? Did you make lots of money from doing a book?

The short and honest answer is no. People seem to think that having a book means you've struck it rich, but it's just not so. I don't want to discourage anyone from going for it, but I don't want anyone to go for it with the wrong idea of what is involved. If your goal is to become rich, play the lottery, marry wealthy…. If you are proud of your work, are able to attract an agent or publisher and want to extend your name and broaden your exposure, then maybe a book makes sense to do. But it will require an enormous commitment of your time and require you to collaborate on your ideas. Doing a craft book is an enormous undertaking that can take anywhere from three to nine months (or longer) for you to complete. There are numerous revisions with your editor(s), white-knuckle deadlines (being creative on demand ain't easy), release dates that extend well beyond a year (or longer) after you've turned in your project. And you don't get paid until after the advance has been earned back from sales of the book. Which might not happen.

It's incredibly exciting and rewarding to see your work in print, but getting to that point takes a very, very long time and the efforts of many people. And, the publishing industry has gone through major changes in the last several years due to the proliferation of desktop publishing and the internet. Advances are dwindling and the book tour is no longer. Most authors are completely on their own with regard to promoting their titles. Only very, very rarely do authors get sent on book tours.

I was lucky. My books have done well and I actually received royalty checks from them in the years following their release. But, I re-invested every dime back into my company. Doing books was a way for me to extend my reach in ways my publisher could (that I couldn't) and I put any money that was earned back into my company. There were no Carrie Bradshaw "lookie-at-this-$25K-check-my-publisher-just-floated-me" moments. Instead, it was more like "$3,000-is-the-most-money-I've-ever-seen-in-my-life-so-I-better-be smart-about-what-I-do-with-it". (It went into my business.)

It's extremely difficult, and becoming increasingly difficult to land a book deal with a bona-fide publishing house unless you already have an established name as an author, TV personality, or designer. Which, if you view books as a way to establish your name, presents a very chicken-and-egg conundrum. The good news is that it's much easier now to demonstrate that you have a readership. If you can show that you have a huge following on your blog, twitter, facebook, or if you've managed to get an article published in a magazine ("Tattoo Your Towels" was the name of the first how-to article I wrote), then you might have a strong start to attracting an editor for a project.

As for how it happened to me, it's kind of like explaining how a person got hit by lightning. The short answer is: I was extremely fortunate to be approached by a publisher who wanted me specifically for a project. Then, deal in hand, I got myself a literary agent. But this didn't happen before I was rejected numerous times, including initial rejections from my current publisher and my own agent. No kidding! (I don't hold it against them, though.)

Why did you go to an agent if you already had a project offered to you?

A literary agent can read a contract in ways that you can't, is bad cop to your good cop if any issues arise between you and your editor, and they know how to negotiate for more money. If you don't really know the ins and outs of publishing, you want a good agent by your side guiding you through the process to help you avoid any pitfalls in the process. However, I know plenty of authors who work successfully without agents. It's a personal choice, understanding that your agent will typically get at least 15% of anything a publisher pays you.

So do your research: research literary agents who work in the area you want to write about, research publishers big and small. Ask yourself: what is my book about? Why would it be unique? Why would I be the best person to write it? Why do I want this or that publisher to put it out? Would they be the best publisher for this title? Will it fit in with their other books? Because they will ask you those very questions themselves. If you can't paint a strong and clear picture then, hello slush pile (where orphaned proposals go to die).

Your kits designs have such a unique and individual look. Have your designs or ideas ever been copied/ripped off? What happened?

The short answer is yes, many times. To be clear: I'm talking about established businesses reproducing and manufacturing my work without permission or pay, not small hand makers. I'm not talking about some genuinely innocent or honestly independent and small designer selling product with my designs on them, made by hand. Those instances result in one-on-one emails to say "Maybe you weren't aware that I have a licensing program?" In those instances, I've never had a problem, and I don't make a big deal out of it.

This is always a hard one to discuss because some people see the copying, and some don't. And, sometimes it really is, and sometimes it's not. Sometimes it's intentional, sometimes it's not. If your work is successful and popular, it's going to be copied. By reason of being influential on popular culture, by people being "inspired" by what you do and running away with it themselves, and businesses seeing your creative work as a fast way for them to make money—and just not bother paying you for it. It's only been the times when an established business willfully, knowingly, copied my work (ie: purchasing my patterns and then providing them to a paid artist on their staff in order to make product they would sell themselves) that I've taken legal action. It's not fun. And there is no "get a big settlement" when it happens. The process is long and extremely time-consuming and difficult. It is never a good thing. If you have to resort to legal action, you've already lost time, money, and initial market exposure. And while it's true that you can't stop someone from ripping you off in the first place, you can work to discourage it and avoid it from happening from the start. I'm always very disappointed whenever I hear any artist or designer say they think it would be good for their careers to get their work ripped off by some large company. It's not. Everyone loses. It stops you from doing your most important work, and it's very stressful and emotionally draining.

Since I started my company, I have had to take legal action to stop three clothing lines that appeared in national chains with my designs on them, three trademark disputes that were settled (amicably) and address one instance of published plagiarism. Fun, right? In each instance with the clothing companies, the company had purchased the patterns directly from my website and they were simply put into production. In another instance, my patterns were purchased quietly by the company's CEO and staff and used in the research and development of a new "business unit" of the company that looked like they were a new company, run by just a couple of young women introducing a new line of embroidery patterns. I (and the public) began to notice the way-too-similar similarities but they were not aware that they were a multi-million-dollar company of multiple artists and staff that had been in business for 20 years.

So, according to popular belief, I should be rich from settlements after being ripped off so many times, but every dime we settled for went to the lawyers. So why do it? Because copyright is a use-it-or-lose-it thing. You have to actively protect your copyright in order to maintain your right to protect it.

Wow—any other scary tales to tell?

Several years ago I was approached by a major craft manufacturing corporation. I was asked to design and license a series of embroidery kits and patterns that they would manufacture with my brand. Working with them was something I had to consider very carefully and seriously. It was not something I just leapt at, clapping my hands with joy. I had to consider: How would this impact smaller businesses that carry my product? How could this help my company? Would my customers and fans think I was doing it to sell out? Would the quality of my product be maintained? Are they paying me enough to hand over this work? (The answers to these questions would turn out to be: negatively; bigger market; possibly; unknown at the time (no); and hardly.)

But, I respected that this company wanted to bring in an independent designer on the merits of their work, which I took as a sign of a good company. But just as much, I also feared that if I didn't work with them, they might just rip me off anyway. It felt like an "if-you-can't-beat-em-join-em" decision.

I was flown to their headquarters and met with staff and their most senior people for hours. We had signed confidentiality contracts so we could freely share ideas in a daylong meeting with the understanding these ideas were not to leave the room or be used for anything other than the work I would do with them. They previewed their upcoming product lines for me, and then we spent more than a month carefully negotiating the contract. For me, this was a big, big deal.

After we agreed to move forward, I began working with a small team of people, the most important of whom were in my initial meeting, who would make the line happen, in manufacturing terms, while I did what I'd always dreamed of: nothing but the creative part.

What I was unaware of (because they were careful not to tell me) was that the main person I was working with on color choices, design concepts, and basically, all creative aspects was one of their in-house designers. I was never told this person was a staff designer, which is a very big no-no. Had I known this, I never would have agreed to work with that person or share creative ideas with him. In-house staff designers are generally not an independent designer's friend. They've earned a deserved reputation for plucking ideas from independent designers to churn out as their own ideas for the company that's cutting their paycheck. Of course, there are countless talented and ethical designers staffed by companies that come by their talents honestly and keep major brands unique and lively with their often anonymously produced, creative contributions. But unfortunately, the pressures from above are great and in-house designers have to seek "inspiration" elsewhere.

Months later, the protoypes for me line with the company debuted at a very large trade show. This is a show not open to the public, where retailers can view product samples and place orders for their stores. It's also a place where competitors' may look at your goods and might produce knockoffs or even try to steal samples. When I arrived at the company's booth, excited to see my line in person and be the smiling face endorsing it, but I was stunned by how poorly my line had been executed. I immediately recognized that it didn't reflect my input or the work I had been told was done. I was crestfallen. And confused—this company successfully produced licensed lines of other designers—so why was mine so horribly bungled? The samples looked bad, the packaging was unfinished, but I had to hide my disappointment and smile for buyers. Then it got worse.

On the second day of the show, I discovered samples that the company's reps seemed to be hiding from me, of "hip" stitching embroidery kits. They weren't on display like the others were. (Remember, my initial meeting with them included a preview of all their upcoming lines, and this one was never shown to me.) As soon as I saw them, I asked who designed them, because the work was so similar to my own, and I wasn't aware of any other embroidery designers doing what I do. And clearly, far more time and effort had gone into this mystery line. And, hey, wasn't that an idea I shared in our meeting? Who made these?

After witnessing my discovery of the samples, the head of my team scrambled over and, in a laugh-it-off kind of way, said the kits were made by the person on my team. I felt my stomach drop to the floor. I couldn't believe it. It was coming together and falling apart all at the same time. I was furious and panicking inside. I found a way to say that I was not OK with this. But I was told with nervous reassurances that "these won't even go into manufacture" and "we don't even want this person spending time doing this! They're supposed to be working on *your* line!" Translation: We're blowing off your line and putting your concept into a company line under a staff designer's name so we won't have to pay you and thus make more money for the company.

So what happened next?

A few months later, the other line was released. My kits had languished in unfinished production, key members of my team had started leaving the company, and I was left twisting in the wind with unanswered e-mails from the company and phone meetings resulting in someone's voicemail. I refocused my time and efforts on Sublime Stitching. I had lost a lot of time and energy sorely needed there. I just wanted to forget I'd ever worked with this company. But things were about to take another unexpected turn.

The company moved forward to produce my kits without my further involvement or approval. I was shocked when samples were suddenly sent to me. I held in my hands a product line that turned out to be slapped together with cheap materials, transfers that didn't transfer, bad graphics, and spelling mistakes throughout the instructions. Agreed layouts, wording, and packaging had been ignored. Now I really panicked—at the thought of these kits appearing in stores with my name, my face and the company's mistakes and misdeeds all over them.

I had worked more than a year to make this line happen, trying my best to ensure the quality and protect the good name of my company. This could destroy all of that! I called the most senior contact I had at the company and told her we had a problem. And then I did the only thing I could do: I explained that I wouldn't endorse the kits or sell them myself and wouldn't be at the next trade show to help promote them. I also made it clear that I felt I had been deliberately misled while they produced a competing product, and so long as they continued with it, our relationship would end.

After some firm conversations, they agreed to pull and destroy all the inventory, which meant a sickening amount of money had been wasted. Down the toilet. Bye-bye. Money that my little company could only dream of having to invest in its own growth with quality product.

I walked away and discussed pursuing legal action against this company with my lawyer, who agreed there was a strong case for being defrauded. But I made the wrenchingly difficult decision to move on and not waste further time (and money) pursuing legal action.

I wanted to share this story to let people know that this sort of thing really does happen and that I lived through it. I don't consider this the worst thing that's happened to my business, either. The situation could have been much, much worse had I not carefully negotiated the terms before anything went wrong and refused to sign it before we detailed only what work the contract encompassed (an initial contract I was handed covered a wide swath of my intellectual property, including "all future designs"). I learned a lot from this experience and am really glad it's far behind me.

A lot of small businesses and designers dream of having a large company come along, like a knight in shining armor and make them bigger or take over their manufacturing and "get them into the big stores." But it really doesn't work that way, especially if you have an identity and level of quality you don't want to see undergo drastic changes. It's far more complicated and risky. This experience only caused me to re-double my efforts of independent growth, which have been far more successful and definitely more gratifying.

Jenny Hart's
Top Ten Tips for Crafty Business Success

1) Be realistic about what you can and can't do.

2) Envision your goals and remain focused on them.

3) Know when to say yes (or no) to opportunities that will take you away from your original plan.

4) Do your best work.

5) Do your taxes, pay your bills on time and learn to keep books.

6) Don't assume anything will go as planned.

7) Be open to constructive criticism, feedback and be prepared to make changes along the way, at any time.

8) Understand your business better than anyone else. Know it inside and out.

9) Go easy on yourself and know when it's time to take a break.

10) Do it only for as long as you enjoy it. The enjoyment will show in your work.

EMILY PEACOCK

Name: **Emily Peacock**

Company Name: **Emily Peacock**

Founded in: **2007**

Location: **Buckinghamshire, UK**

No. of Employees: **3**

Website: **www.emilypeacock.com**

Emily Peacock trained as a graphic and packaging designer and worked in a typography and typesetting studio before turning to the medium of textiles, and particularly tapestry. UK-based Emily's range of tapestry and cushion kits are instantly recognizable for their bold, fun and quirky designs, and have been featured on many TV shows, magazines and sold to crafters around the world.

Please tell us a bit about your career/background and how the Emily Peacock kit range came about?

I worked for many years in Graphic design, learning 'on the job' in design studios, typesetters and packaging design companies. Although I really enjoyed my work, I used to go home and stitch and sew—this was my real passion and I always had projects of one type or another on the go.

I think I was like a lot of people—I really felt I had something creative to give but I couldn't find exactly what it was. I used to try many different ideas and just end up frustrated. Looking back, I think my thought process was that I had to come up with something that fell in with an existing market, rather than creating something new.

I moved with my husband and children to France in 2003 and it was a tough time. We had very little income and I found it hard to settle. In short, I felt lonely and lost and began to wonder what I was made of. In the UK it was easier to be distracted by my working life, friends and family and delay finding what it was I wanted to do, but in France I felt I had no excuse and if I didn't grab the moment I would maybe feel that I had let myself down. I decided to order some wools and start playing. I experimented with different wools and canvases and decided I liked cross stitch on canvas the best. I then started to make the sort of cushions I would want in my home.

We returned to England in 2007 with very little money, no jobs to go to and just this idea of selling my cushion designs as needlepoint kits. It seemed that every door I knocked on opened and I think it's because my product was original and coincided with the revolution in craft taking place in the UK. Within no time my work was appearing in magazines and my kits were being sold in Liberty.

Describe the space you work from? How do you make it inspiring as well as functional?

Since we came back from France we have rented houses. In 4 years we have moved four times as we needed bigger and bigger properties for me to work in. In my current house I have a studio to work out of. I think there is a tendency to imagine designers wafting round in their creative space, sucking a pencil waiting for the muse to strike, but with me it's hard graft and functionality. I keep files of images that inspire me, but I mostly carry my ideas in my head.

Do you produce all of your kits yourself? How did you source all the components and find the right parts? Do you personally make each kit yourself?

I used Appleton's wools years before I started producing kits. I love their color range and the fact that they do 2 weights of wool and so that choice was obvious to me. My knowledge of needlework was quite extensive through years of teaching myself, so I knew exactly where to go for wool and canvas.

I was making all the kits myself but demand became far too high. I outsource winding wool and have it returned by the bin bag. My assistant Katie cuts the canvases and sometimes I lend a hand at putting kits together depending on how busy I am. I mainly sell direct to customers through my website and do not get involved in large orders as I simply do not have the set up. Having said that, even direct sales are becoming too much for me and for my wool supplier, so I am looking to completely change the way I operate and maybe involve a fulfillment company.

How did you work out what prices to retail your kits at? Is there a formula that you use?

I worked out my prices on store mark-up. In other words I added up all my costs (including my time), added a small realistic profit that I would be happy with if large quantities were ordered and then worked out a typical store mark-up. My kits are not cheap but they are competitively priced for this type of product

Your online store is fab! Please discuss your experiences/thoughts/tips on managing stock/shipping to customers/accepting returns etc? Do you also sell on Etsy?

Thanks! Shipping to customers and accepting returns is simple. I ship everything signed for and very little is ever returned. I am happy to accept returns up to 60 days from date of order. Stock is another matter. I have had huge issues with the dyers keeping up with my demand. I buy my wool by bags of 200 hanks and try to ensure I have plenty in stock but I have had to state on my website that colors in my designs may vary. I think of all the tasks involved in running a business, stock is the biggest headache.

Etsy is a dream. It's so simple to set up and keeps excellent records of what has been sold and which product has had the most views and so on, plus it has a huge global audience that is not easy to reach through other methods. There is a small charge for each transaction but when you bear in mind that you are effectively getting a store front where people can search for your product by name and type, it's a very inexpensive way to get started.

You now have an assistant—Katie. How did you know it was time to start employing someone rather than continue to juggle all the balls yourself? How did you know you could afford it?

Katie is in fact my sister. We have a great relationship and really see eye to eye design-wise. I needed an assistant for a while as I seemed to be constantly drowning in work and my turnover had been consistently high enough to warrant hiring help. Katie seemed the obvious choice.

Trade Fairs—An expensive, but necessary tool? Do you need to do these to get into shops?

I am not looking to increase my trade sales at the moment, so these fairs are not suitable for my business. I have done some consumer shows in London—*Stitch and Craft* at Olympia and *The Knitting & Stitching Show* at Alexander Palace—but the cost of the show versus the amount of direct sales I get is not really worth the time.

You sell directly to the public via your website AND wholesale to lots of shops and online stores. What % of your business would you say is wholesale vs retail. Is it really worth selling to shops when the margins are much lower than selling directly to your customers?

I don't wholesale my kits to lots of shops. I sell to Liberty and a couple of small shops but I have had to draw the line as demand was too high. I sell 98% of my kits through my website and Etsy and the other 2% through other outlets. As long as I have to be in charge of production, I will not be increasing my trade sales. I feel I have an original idea and I am not willing to work late into the night for very small profit to fulfill trade orders. If my production methods change then I will happily do as much wholesale as I can.

Cash flow/finances—one of the biggest challenges of a small business owner. How have you financed the growth of your company—did you have to approach the banks for loans? How do you make sure retailers pay you on time?

I have never had a loan or borrowed money for my business. I started small and paid for what I could afford and always invested profits into stock. My circle of stockists is very small, I have a good working relationship with all of them and I have never had a problem with payment.

You have a fantastic book out—'*Adventures In Needlework*'. So you must be rich, right?

You don't get rich by having a book out and my decision to do a book came from the same place as my decision to start a business—it was simply something

I wanted to do. I can honestly say that money has never been a factor in any decision I have ever made. If you have an idea it has to come from a place of personal passion, belief and integrity, definitely not from 'what would make me rich?'

I have been approached by a few publishers. My book was published by GMC and their offer came at a time when I was working with my friend Jessica Aldred from The Royal School of Needlework. We were discussing doing 'something' together, so we decided to write a good technical book. You are paid a small advance whilst you compile the book and then you receive royalties based on sales. The book is a collaboration and so there are elements of me and elements of Jessica in it. What is extremely challenging is the deadlines you are given. We produced the book in 9 months which was quite a feat given the amount of work involved and I could not have possibly done it alone. If I were to do a book again I would take my time, probably just stick to cross stitch and canvas work and only approach a publisher once I had sufficient material.

Your kits designs have such a unique and individual look. Have your designs or ideas ever been copied/ripped off? What happened? What did you do? Discuss...

When I began my business my methods were unique—there was no one using 2 counts of canvas and 2 types of wool in counted cross stitch. The needlepoint kit designs available tended to be traditional and I believe I was the first to introduce lettering adopted from my years in Graphic Design, along with my bright color palette. I have had my methods directly copied and my modern design ideas adopted. It never feels good to have this happen to you. You have arrived at the place you are in through your own thoughts and you have taken risks and gone through finding the strength and confidence to be there, so when someone takes these ideas from you it is not only immoral, it feels like a very personal theft.

I delight in designers contributing their own modern take on needlepoint and this is by no means a turf war, but directly copying methods and ideas is shameless and not to be tolerated. That sounds strong, but protecting original thought is something I feel very strongly about and I make no apologies for being vocal about it. If you like the way someone thinks, commission them.

You can protect your designs through organizations such as ACID, but there are many situations where there is not much you can do apart from confront. Of course thieves tend to also be liars and will deny any wrong doing, so the best thing you can do is to put your efforts into producing good, original work.

What do you wish you'd know back when you started out?

The biggest mistake I have ever made was to say yes to too many things. I think there's a tendency when you begin a business to be so flattered by any attention you get and so worried that it could all dry up tomorrow, that you say yes to everything. I see things differently now and I try to put myself first, protect myself and put my energy in the right places. In the past I have been in a position where I have had to force designs out whilst dealing with huge quantities of orders and that never works and I end up feeling depleted and that I've let myself down.

The other thing I would say is to trust your own instincts. If you really believe you have something to offer, then go with it. I have been told by many well-meaning individuals what I should be designing and how I should be running my business and I have nodded politely then gone and done exactly what feels right for me. You will be offered all sorts of well meaning advice, but nobody can think for you and no one else is living your life. You have to be single-minded and not swayed by fear and opinion.

And finally...what does the future hold for Emily Peacock...any exciting plans you'd like to share?

That's a hard one, it reminds me of the expression "if you want to make God laugh, tell him your plans." I couldn't have envisaged the path I've been down—all the great experiences I've had and the wonderful people I've met. I will always be a needlework devotee, but would like to explore it in different forms. I would like more design time so I am working towards moving production to a place that takes the pressure off me and can fulfill trade orders. I have also started running workshops and these have been so enjoyable and I have had such great feedback that I really want to do more of these. The main thing is to make decisions that keep needlework moving forward and make people inspired enough to give it a try.

Name: **Julie Jackson**

Company Name: **Subversive Cross Stitch**

Founded in: **2003**

Location: **Dallas, Texas, USA**

No. of Employees: **1**

Website: **www.subversivecrossstitch.com / www.kittywigs.com**

Subversive Cross Stitch is the brainchild of Julie Jackson, and began in the spring of 2003 as a form of anger management therapy when dealing with a mean idiot boss!

Her twisted take on the traditional medium of cross stitch soon gained tons of attention, and she now produces a range of Subversive Cross Stitch kits and patterns, and is the author of a Subversive Cross Stitch book, which has been translated into several languages.

Julie's other business, Kitty Wigs—a crazy and unique range of wigs for cats—has also attracted worldwide press attention and inspired a best-selling book "Glamourpuss". Julie is based in Dallas, Texas.

How would you describe Subversive Cross Stitch to those unfamiliar with your fabulousness?

It's great art therapy; a creative way to turn frustration into snarky, frame-able art!

Tell us how the idea came about and what you were doing for a living at the time?

I was working in a horrible office for an even more horrible boss and going out of my mind. I decided to stop by a craft store and find a creative way to express myself, so I bought a flowery cross stitch kit and after I stitched the border I replaced the sappy sentiment in the center with the word "fuck". It felt great.

Did you continue to work while you launched the business? How long was it before you took the leap to working on this full time?

I had no idea it would turn into a business, I just put a few pieces online to share with friends and the internet found me. The interest was so great that I decided I'd better find a way to let people make their own. I immediately set up an e-news option so I could reach those visitors again and started selling kits within a couple of days. I had been a freelance copywriter working at home before, so this gave me the courage (if not the money) to quit the awful job and go back to freelancing. I could never afford it, really, I just DID it. I just knew I couldn't stay at that soul-crushing job another day.

Describe the space you work from? Any tips for those working from their home?

I work at home in a small office and have a shipping station in a separate room for when I have help. I have great hopes of turning our garage into a proper dream space, but that'll take more money and time than I have right now. I have all my favorite things around me in my office and it's a really fun space, but it's also ridiculously chaotic. I'm sure it's absolutely nothing like people might imagine the headquarters of Subversive and Kitty Wigs to look like!!

I produce all the kits myself except for the foreign language kits, which are produced by Noted. I had zero experience in this area when I started out, so I just did a lot of research and started out small. I outsourced kit making for large orders like Urban Outfitters and Target's Red Hot Shop, but mostly I get some help in and we crank it out. Before the recession hit, I had a couple of helpers, but lately things have been tough so I try to save all the money I can while still keeping my customers happy. It is a great challenge, especially during the holidays. And this year, I have a deal going with Thrillist Rewards, Subversive is in the Daily Candy gift guide and the Kitty Wigs book (Glamourpuss) is coming out as an eBook right before the holidays, so it's ridiculously insane around here with orders!

The most important thing to me is customer service. I believe in the Neiman Marcus kind of service—I strive to go above and beyond to keep my customers happy. I never argue, they're always right, and I will return or ship a second order without question. I really want my customers to be happy, it's the most important thing to me, and I find that honesty is the best policy. If someone's order slipped through the cracks and wasn't sent, I tell them and I apologize and try to make it right plus give them something extra. My main rule is to be honest at all times, especially when I just plain screw up. I would be nothing without my customers, they mean the world to me. That said, it's incredibly hard to keep up with emails this time of year so sometimes I'm late in shipping or responding to inquiries. All I can do is wait for the economy to improve so I can afford more help and in the meantime, I do the best I can. People are amazingly patient and understanding, nine times out of ten at least.

As for online stores, there are SO many more options today than when I started out. If I were just starting now, I would try Etsy first. Besides selling kits directly on my website, I sell supplies on Etsy because it's easy to keep track of stock (which is something I haven't had time to build into my site yet). Also, I have a PDF shop through Big Cartel which allows me to stay out of the process and customers receive the PDFs via email almost instantly. That's a pretty swell deal.

This was definitely a conscious decision from the outset. I don't want to be the face of Subversive Cross Stitch—I want people to take the idea and make it their own. It's not about me. I think it's absolutely possible to launch any business online without face time, especially these days. In all the business I've done with big companies I've never had a face-to-face meeting.

I've had so many other jobs that involved travel, endless meetings and pointless conference calls, picking up the phone and constantly interrupting work—I swore to myself that I would never do business that way. And I don't.

I don't talk on the phone unless I have to or want to; and if I'm writing, I don't answer the phone or the door at all! If I did, I would never get anything done, and I have quite a heavy load of things to do! Once the New York Times was going to send a reporter to Dallas to interview me and take photos as part of a bigger story about crafters and I completely balked at the idea. Why take all that time and nervous preparation to go through something I really didn't want to go through and that probably would be edited out, anyway? In the end, the story was cancelled, but I had stood by my guns, though it was a hard call. It's not because I didn't care or didn't recognize the value, but everything in me was telling me it would turn out badly and be a miserable experience. I have to follow my instincts completely. The times I went against my gut feeling and did something for press—those were the times I've not only felt like a whore but I allowed way too much stress into my life. So it is definitely a conscious business strategy and not at all a lack of caring.

You've been lucky enough to gain tons of press coverage for your kits and patterns. Do you do your own PR?

The press I've gotten has been pure luck. I've been in advertising and copywriting for years—I can't tell you how many press releases I've written in my lifetime—but I never set out with a formal plan for my businesses. In fact, I only wrote one press release when Subversive took off. I sent it to Bust (my favorite magazine of all time) and ReadyMade because they were the only ones covering DIY stuff at the time. After that, it was just sheer luck and a lot of persistence and awareness of the craft scene that was building.

The one thing I've learned about press is that they will always get something wrong. You just have to accept that and roll with it. If it's online they can change it, but if it's in print it's there forever. I've never sent out free samples but, remember, when I started out there was not a huge interest in DIY so there are a lot more opportunities now. I think the more you can do online in establishing yourself as a brand and building up your audience is probably the best way to start. I didn't even have Facebook and Twitter when I started, and those are amazing tools you can harness these days.

As far as press turning into sales, you never know. It's no longer an ego boost, really—I spend more energy bracing myself for what they're going to get wrong! For example, recently I was asked to stitch the cover art for Parade magazine. All the PR people I know went nuts about the distribution, etc. and what a big deal it was. I picked up the paper that day and didn't see any credits. A few of us looked and none of us saw credits. I was disappointed but not surprised. I talked to Parade on the Monday morning and they pointed out that the credits were running vertically in the "gutter" on the story page. So I got out a magnifying glass and, sure enough, there they were. But, really, who's going to go to that much trouble to find out who stitched the cover art? You have to manage your expectations with press and always keep your ego in check. Everyone is out there doing their own thing, and if you happen to cross their radar, you're really lucky. But don't expect them to get the details right when a hundred other things are on their radar, too.

You're an author too with 2 great books out (*Subversive Cross Stitch* and *Glamourpuss*—both on Chronicle Books)! Most creative crafters would dream of securing a book deal—how did you get yours?

Oh, books. Well, the first thing you need to know about doing books is that they will never really make a lot of money. The second thing is, get a literary agent to show you the ropes and help you navigate the system because it can be really complicated and confusing. It's an entirely different business.

Books are great as vehicles for your brand and to get press, but people seem to think that if you have a book out, you're counting your cash and living the easy life. Not true. I know so many people who have done craft books and we're all in the same boat. That said, it's still a great opportunity and a lot of fun. I adore the folks at Chronicle, they're so much fun to work with and they really go to bat for their authors. If you're passionate about your subject matter, doing a book is a great adventure. If you just want to make a bunch of money, you're in it for the wrong reasons.

I got the Subversive book deal through a book packager who contacted me about creating a book of patterns and then they shopped the concept to various publishers at a book fair and Chronicle bought it. In both cases, I got book deals because I already had the brand out there and had a lot of name recognition, so I can't really speak to pitches, though I did have to put together a pitch for Kitty Wigs, which was fun. If you're in that situation, be as creative as you can and think outside the box. And don't be discouraged. I know so many people who have great book ideas but haven't gotten published despite several pitches. This doesn't mean your idea stinks, it's all about timing and money. Don't take it personally, just keep trying!

The best thing about the books I've done is seeing them translated to other languages: the Subversive book came out in Dutch and Glamourpuss came out in Japanese and Korean! That was really exciting. Though selling foreign rights is not a cash cow, either. The other thing about books is that it takes a very long time to see money from them because everything takes a long time in the publishing world. They have to wait for sales figures and 90 days for returns, etc…it goes on and on. I thought I was patient, but it requires incredible patience—another reason not to be in it for the money.

That said, I'm really happy to tell you that the Kitty Wigs book, Glamourpuss, recently sold through its advance. This means that we sold enough tens of thousands of books to earn out our advance, which means it's a success and that sometime next year I'll be looking at royalties! I finally feel like a successful author. It only took about a decade, plus tons of work and a whole lot of interviews and press!

Julie Jackson's
Top Ten Tips for Crafty Business Success

1) Do your own thing. Even if 20 people are doing the exact same thing, your interpretation will be unique. There's lots of room for everyone.

2) Trust your instincts completely. If it feels wrong, it probably is.

3) Paypal is awesome.

4) If you don't already subscribe to Bust magazine, you must. They have had their finger on the whole DIY scene from the beginning and they do it like no one else. It's almost like they're psychic. It's the only magazine I get that I have to read immediately and I end up marking about half the pages to look at later. www.bust.com

5) Don't worry about what other people think of you or your idea. Can you imagine the feedback I would have gotten if I'd asked people whether or not I should pursue a business creating wigs for cats? It never would have left the ground. Just do your own thing. Also, there will be haters but in the end they always self-destruct.

6) Spend as much time as you can online finding people that truly inspire you. Write to them, tap into their energy, find out what makes them tick, and ask them for advice. Don't be shy.

7) Try to keep up with the Craft magazine blog. If there's something going on in the craft world, they're on top of it. http://blog.craftzine.com

8) Read Hugh MacLeod's books, "Ignore Everybody" and "Evil Plans". He's an illustrator so his books are brief, fun and madly inspiring: http://gapingvoid.com/books

9) If you're not looking forward to what you're working on, move on and try something else. Your heart's got to be into what you're doing or you haven't found your niche yet.

10) Go for it. Don't spend too much time over-thinking and worrying about whether things will work or not. Just get something out there right now that you can build on. Whatever you start with will change a million times, so just START.

Amy Karol

Name: **Amy Karol**

Business: **Author and Crafty Entrepreneur**

Founded in: **2002**

Location: **Portland, Oregon, USA**

Website: **www.amykarol.com**

So, what's my deal? I make stuff.

I write books, draw, paint, cook, sew, parent young children, try to do yoga more often than not, and am constantly using my creativity to both express myself and not take life too seriously.

I have had the pleasure of writing some sewing books, *Bend-the-Rules Sewing: The Essential Guide to a Whole New Way to Sew* (Potter Craft 2007), which is currently in its fourth printing, and *Bend the Rules with Fabric: Fun Sewing Projects with Stencils, Stamps, Dye, Photo Transfers, Silk Screening, and More* (Potter Craft 2009).

Before having my three lovely daughters and moving back to my hometown of Portland, Oregon with my husband, I worked in Seattle as a commercial interior designer, using my handy degree in interior architecture from University of Oregon with a fine art, architecture and costume construction minor, which I received in 1996.

I love trying new things, which has led me to explore all kinds of shenanigans. I have sewn wedding dresses, printed custom invitations, made short films, recorded a few songs, done a little commercial radio work, written terrible short plays, had art shows in various galleries featuring my paintings, monoprints, and large and small quilts—a little bit of a lot of things.

You're a busy bee, with your fingers in a lot of creative pies! How did you go from being a commercial interior designer to being a well-known crafty whizz kid?

Thanks! I do have a lot going on at once. I think the interior design, in the overall arc of my life, was short. 6 years of school and 5 years working, and during that time I was always painting, sewing, and making things, so it wasn't like I was only a designer and then a stuff-maker. They co-existed. I have been a crafter and made things, and I guess I did always figure I'd make money being creative, but there has never been a clear vision of exactly how. It's always been an evolving thing.

Describe the space you work from….Do you work from home? How do you make your space inspiring as well as functional? Any tips for those working from their home?

I do work from home now and have for some time. I used to have an art studio, mostly because our apartments were always too small for me to get messy in. Since having kids, I have worked from home. I try to keep the room clean and organized, but I try to be realistic. It's rare I can work alone, so if I have really important stuff the kids can't get into, it goes on high shelves or out of sight. That's easier than saying "no" a hundred times.

You're also a mom to 3 lovely daughters who you homeschool. Wow—how on earth do you find the time for all your creative pursuits!?

I do have 3 girls! Sadie 9, Delia, 7, and Lydia, 4. And the time is tight, I will admit that. And it has changed. In many ways, I had more time when they were younger, but now, much of my day is spent teaching them, so I work in early mornings, evenings, or weekends. It's a balance and can be tricky. I try not to do too much, but it's hard when I am excited by a new project. My enthusiasm can be hard to manage at times.

Tell us about mailorder, your online craft club? What a cool idea? How did this get started, and how has it changed over the years?

Thank you, it's been so fun. I got the idea to do a craft club. I have always loved mail, and created new issues 4 times a year. Then 3 times a year, and then less, and now the new issues are only PDF. It was so great designing the paper goods to mail, but after spending weeks stuffing and mailing every month, it was too much, so I switched to a digital format. A new one comes out about once a year. It's evolved with me—when I started, the girls were just babies. The great thing about a PDF is I only have to design it once and can sell it forever and never run out of supplies.

You also have a hugely popular blog—*Angry Chicken*. When did you first get into blogging? Why do you blog?

I started the blog in 2006 and why I blog changes, but I think in a nutshell it's a way to connect with people and share creative energy. There was no money to be made when I started, not just by blogging. No advertising, just a group of creative types supporting each other. As a stay at home mom desperate for adult interaction, it was a life saver. I already had a site up selling my artwork and quilts and handmade wares, so the blog was just a journal. But, after a bit, it became clear that the website could only do so much and keeping people informed as to what I was doing and what I sold was perfect to blog about. Then of course, it changed a bit of what the blog was. It still is a way to connect, but it's also a way to tell the world what I have to offer, and to sell. And it's a great place to get ideas about new items to sell depending on the feedback I get from the blog. So it's all mixed up together.

You also have another great website—*Tie One On*—dedicated to the love of making Aprons! Unlike many popular crafty bloggers these days, you don't sell adverts on your blog or websites, yet you must spend hours sharing all your tips and cool projects with the world and could easily generate an income for all this hard work. What were your reasons/motivation for not commercializing this part of your output?

Yes, well, this can be a tricky subject, but I think at the end of the day, it's just a better fit for me to not sell ads. Having said that, I am an associate with some companies, and I also do book/product reviews sometimes, but it's only for items I truly love and am 100% comfortable promoting—but I don't have any paid ads on my site. I am more comfortable selling what I make and design and making money from that, as opposed to directly from ads/blogging. I need to be able to take a break from the blog (I usually take a month off in the summer) and also need to feel I have the freedom on my blog to say whatever I want to and never worry about offending advertisers. Also I think I care too much about my blog to make it that much of a job, if that makes sense. It's too special. This is so personal, however, it's different for everyone. Also, I started blogging when ads weren't really around, so I never had that in my head from the get go, the way so many folks do now.

Congratulations! You're an author too with 2 great books out. Most creative crafters would dream of securing a book deal—how did you get yours?

I was contacted through the work on my blog, but also from my personal art site, Kingpod, which is still around and hasn't changed in 6 years! Writing books is a labor of love. I am so proud of my books and would love to do more when the time/topic is a good fit for me. But, it's not for everyone, a lot like blogging, actually. I would never tell anyone to do it for the money. If you want to be published and have a book in the world, then writing a book is a great way to do that. But, self-publishing is also an option-especially in a digital format. I guess fearlessly analyze why you would want to write a book, and when you figure that out, research if your reason is a realistic expectation. This sounds simple, but can be really hard to do actually.

You've also contributed projects to lots of great magazines and books. When people see someone having such a great profile, they assume they must be making tons of money. Do you get paid for any of this?

I almost never get paid. At all. Pretty much every book I have been in is not paid, or if it is, it's under $100. The magazines sometimes pay a bit more. I do it to support friends that are authors and get myself out there. I say "no" a lot and try to say "yes" to projects I truly want to be a part of, but really, it's not a way to make money. And you have a deadline that you can't control! My worst nightmare! I am smiling as a type this—it's all good, I love contributing when I can, but it's to be a part of the community. I also really love design challenges and think they are fun, so when someone asks me to come up with something for a book/magazine, I often get excited and get a nice creative buzz. The most money I have ever made has just been selling my own patterns/art/designs directly to buyers. I love working with publishers and magazines, but for me, the actual money comes from the direct sales from doing my own thing.

Hmm. no. Think that's enough! The *Tie One On* apron project I have hosted is something I am especially proud of—over the years, there have been more than 1000 aprons that have been made by sewers and submitted for a *Tie One On* theme. That blows my mind and puts a huge grin on my face!

Any advice for others about to embark on their own creative adventure?

This is hard, I have different advice for bloggers, writers, sewers, and designers. So, I guess I will be a bit vague and have the advice be flexible. I know many artists who start to sell and place a lot of rules on themselves. "I will only sell this type of item" or "I am a sewer, I will just sew, not draw and sell art, because I sell only sewn items" the only rules we have are the ones we place on ourselves—and sometimes it's good to re-evaluate what you really want to do.

Also, in a very honest way, I always ask myself before I sell something "would I buy this?" and if the answer is yes, then okay, but if there is any hesitation, I scrap it and move on. If I wouldn't personally spend my hard-earned money on it, I don't expect anyone else to.

Amy Karol's
Top Ten Tips for Crafty Business Success

1) The golden rule—treat others as you would like to be treated.

2) Never write a business e-mail that you wouldn't be comfortable being made public.

3) Treat your customer with absolute respect, always. Be kind and generous in all situations.

4) Being your own boss is both wonderful and hard. Be nice to yourself, but also critical of your work and admit when it's time to move on to a new idea.

5) Be careful with goals. You might never achieve what you set out to do originally, but acknowledge all the things you have done that you never expected to do.

6) Be very careful working with friends. No business plan is worth trashing a friendship for.

7) If you ever find yourself asking another artist permission to sell an item that looks a lot like theirs, it means you need to come up with something else. If you have to ask—it's too similar.

8) Be generous with what you learn and share tips and experience with other crafters.

9) Try to not react too quickly to anything. E-mails, feedback, criticism, and even success. Just sit back and take a breath before doing anything. A walk always helps.

10) Be aware that success or perceived success can change your relationships. Try to be honest with yourself and others as you go down this road and try not to compare yourself to others.

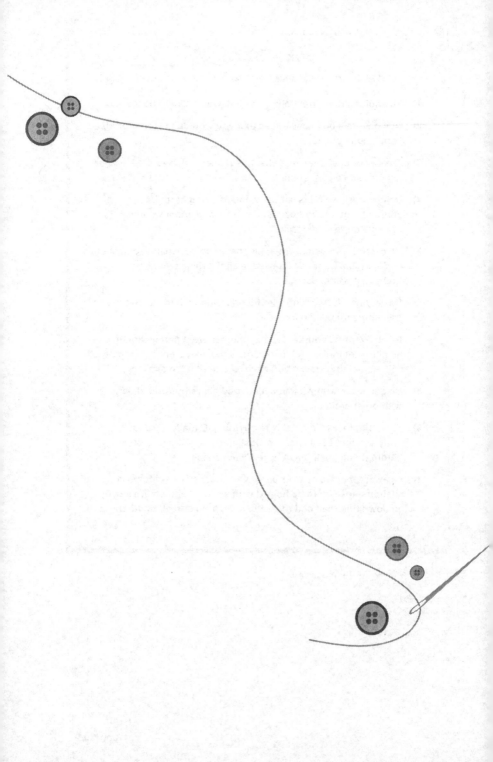

Fashion & Accessories

acorn & will

Name: **Daniella Segal**

Company Name: **acorn & will**

Location: **Surrey, UK**

Website: **www.acornandwill.co.uk**

acorn & will was founded by Surrey, England based crafter Daniella Segal, and is a reflection of her passion for all things vintage.

The acorn & will collection consists of jewelry, hair accessories, cushions and a collection of vintage essentials, all of which are handmade using vintage fabrics and finds.

acorn & will really is a family affair. Danielle's mum Delphine and twin sister Hayley help out at fairs and try out all new products between them. Dad John is always ready with advice, and partner Paul is the IT expert, helping to make the acorn & will online store fabulous!

Tell us a bit about your career background, prior to starting acorn & will?

After gaining a history degree, I moved to Australia where I lived for 8 years, and while there I worked as a pharmaceutical sales representative. When I returned to England, I got a job as an account manager for a company that manufactured bedpans and commodes. My days were filled with conducting commode audits! It sounds awful but I really enjoyed it! From there I moved to become an account manager for a company that manufactured surgical gloves and other surgical equipment. I hate the sight of blood and so having to go into the operating theatre during surgery was a real challenge!

Describe the first steps in creating your business—when did you have the idea, what were your aims, and were you working for other people at the time?

Several years ago, a friend of mine was at a loose end and wanted to start a business, but she didn't have any idea of what to sell. I decided that life was too short to don theatre scrubs and do a job that I didn't enjoy—so acorn & will was born! Initially I made and sourced the products and Jenny, my friend, did the 'grown up' things like admin etc. I continued to work full time so that I had an income. We took the plunge and booked a craft show and the range was well received. It was a successful show and shortly afterwards the website was launched. Jenny relocated and I carried on with the business alone. I juggled full time work with acorn & will for a couple of years, and then last year my job role changed, so I decided it was time to leave! It is nearly a year since I left my job to focus on the business and I am really pleased that I took this route.

You hand make a broad range of products—from jewelry to mirrors and hair accessories and cushions. Any ideas how you will upscale to cope with your business growing?

That is a big question and one I am trying to answer at the moment! I currently make all of the fabric covered products myself and I cut out all of the fabrics for the cushions and nail file cases and I have someone who sews them for me. I also finish all of the other products myself and currently it's a case of the more orders that come in, the more hours I work!

Finding the right suppliers is key—what sort of research did you do?

I am lucky in that I have a lovely friend who loves researching and so she has found me the majority of my suppliers online. It is certainly a challenge to find reliable suppliers. I have experienced the frustration of receiving my first delivery of goods only to find that when I place a repeat order, the quality is not the same. I have found that it is worth paying a little bit more for certain components, like the mirrors and earring posts, as the suppliers I have found are reliable.

Please describe the space you work from?

When I first started, I lived in a flat and looking back now I don't know how I managed! Thankfully as the business has grown so has my home. We have an amazing loft space which is fully boarded and I store all of my fabrics and other stock up there. I have a desk up there but I prefer to work downstairs, so I use our dining room table as my work area. I used to have stock all over the house but I am trying to be more organized so that I don't disrupt the whole house!

Your online store is lovely and shows off all of your different ranges—that's a lot of stock! How do you store and ship it all?

I do have a lot of different lines, but luckily everything I sell is small so I am able to store it all in a relatively small space and I don't have to worry about paying for storage. I am incredibly lucky in that I have a twin sister who loves to 'organise'! She has been helping me since being made redundant and it is true to say she has revolutionized my life. Everything is stored neatly in boxes that are labeled and this has really helped. I do ship all of my own orders and in the past I used to ship orders every day, however I have found it is more efficient for me to ship them on Mondays, Wednesdays and Fridays. I have a great local Post Office—when one of the ladies brought me back a present from her holiday, I realized that since leaving work she is the person I see the most of during my working week!

What have been your experiences of Trade Fairs?

Pulse in London was my first trade show and I was so nervous beforehand as I didn't know what to expect, but it surpassed my expectations. Most of those that ordered from me were small independent shops and the majority have been a pleasure to deal with. I kept my minimum order amount low so that people could try out the range without having to invest a lot of money, and I think that this helped to generate orders. You have to speculate to accumulate, and so while the trade shows are costly, Pulse was worth it for me and I plan to do more trade shows.

You also do lots of craft and gift fairs to sell directly to the public. Any tips for those about to do their first craft/gift fair?

Craft and gift fairs can really vary. Before booking a stand at a fair, I would look at what PR the event organizers undertake to promote their event. It stands to reason that the events that are promoted on blogs and in the media get more people through the door. I would say that in my experience they are generally worth the money and it is good to take part in them as you get to meet other sellers and in attending such events I have got some trade customers as a result. It is also good to get your products in front of people so that you can hear their feedback—both good and bad!

Have you had any of your products featured in magazines? If so, do you do this yourself?

I have, and in all cases I have been contacted by the journalists to request the products they wanted to feature. I exhibit at the Country Living Fair in London, which lots of journalists attend, and this has really helped. I started the year wanting to increase the amount of press exposure for acorn & will, and as it is time consuming to contact journalists and follow up with them I decided to hire a PR person. Sadly this didn't work out and so what I have learnt from this is to make sure you hire someone who has a passion for your product, or someone who can at least pretend to be passionate about it. I would also check the track record of any PR person.

What's the best piece of advice you've been given. What do you wish you'd know back when you started out?

It sounds very naive but when I started acorn & will it was about making pretty things, and being creative was the main focus. I have since learnt that this is only a small part of things, and in fact most of my time is now spent dispatching orders, sourcing products and doing admin.

It is a bit clichéd but someone once said to me; 'how do you eat an elephant?', and the answer is 'one bite at a time'!!

This is something that has stood me in good stead. I am impatient by nature but I have taken the decision to grow my business slowly and I have never tried to run before I can walk!

Paisley & Stripes

accessories handmade in san francisco

Name: **Irina Kenderova**

Company Name: **Paisley and Stripes**

Location: **San Francisco, USA**

Website: **www.paisleyandstripes.com**

Irina Kenderova has always loved making things: "small, colorful, beautiful pieces that would give me the joy of that tangible "something". I never seriously thought of making a career of my hobby until one day I stumbled upon some neck tie silk fabric samples. A few hundred pounds of it, that is…The fabrics were colorful, beautiful and, most importantly, held the promise of lots and lots of fun. That day I came home with a car full of samples, and a few months later Paisley & Stripes was born. Now, these samples live a second life as fabulous flower corsages, scarves, clutches and stoles as well as hair accessories. Best of all, they are all truly one-of-a-kind!"

Tell us a little about Paisley and Stripes, the company. How would you describe what you do?

What do I do? I always laugh and say "I make small exquisite things. Out of nothing." I have a small accessories line—flower brooches, clutches, bracelet cuffs, made from, or at least with, neck tie material.

What did you do before you launched the company? How did you get the idea for Paisley and Stripes?

I have a rather different background. A masters in Economics sent me into consulting for years. Then the kids came, we moved from Vienna, Austria to San Francisco, life changed. But my mother had taught me to sew and knit and do pretty much everything, and I have always hugely enjoyed it—it gives you an immediate satisfaction; quite different from making a Power Point presentation!

I didn't really plan to start a company. I just happened to find a small mountain of neck tie fabric. These were the samples of neck tie material that a tie maker didn't have any use for. They were brand new fabrics in stunning colors, and they said they had no use for them. I just felt that I had to have them! I bought pretty much everything and just "sat" on it—at first, I had no idea what to do with it. I just needed to "save" them. And then it slowly started happening. I often say that there is no substitute for time— ideas take time to come to you, and then it takes time to perfect the product.

I was still working at a large technology company, juggling young children and demanding clients. It was exhausting and most importantly, I wasn't seeing immediate results of my work. Here it is different. You start with a scrap of fabric and an hour later you can have a fabulous clutch or a flower, or something else! And a few days later, there could be people loving your product and giving you money for it. It is much more immediate.

Please describe the place you work from, and how does this differ to when you started out?

Frankly, not much has changed in this respect! I started in my garage, and although we have since moved to a much bigger house, I'm still in the garage—this time a huge one. Let's call it a studio!

Working from home is a wonderful thing—there is no commute and you can keep an eye on the kids.

With the day to day demands of running a business, how do you keep the creative juices flowing and find inspiration for each new collection?

This can be difficult. It is important to change what you are doing on regular basis. For example I could be making clutches for a few weeks and then I would need to stop and not look at them for a while. I might change into making brooches, and even do something completely unrelated. Exploring areas outside of your immediate realm sometimes gives you new ideas too. Accessories/gifts are more or less a seasonal business, so if one plans ahead, one can have the time to rest and do something else!

Your products are stocked in stores across the San Francisco area—how did you achieve this? Any tips for others looking to approach retailers?

A lot of it was just plain cold-calling. When I had a store I really wanted to be in, I just called, visited and got hold of the buyer. Some of it was through shows (retail as well as wholesale). And sometimes people with stores have seen my product on friends or family and called me up. The product is the first and most important thing—a fabulous product will find its way into people's hands. You want the repeat sales, not just one time try-out.

Pricing the product right is always helpful when starting a new account. Offer a quantity discount, or free shipping, or offer (at least at the beginning) to exchange the unsold items for new ones after 60 days. But never do a commission—people need to have their skin in the game as well.

I am still both, the creative part as well as the sales part, but having sales reps is very helpful. Finding a partner who can run the sales part simply helps the bottom line. Concentrate on what you love doing and find somebody who loves the other part!

Your corsages and cuffs are all made by hand—do you do everything yourself?

Yes, everything still is and will remain made by hand. My prices are relatively high and this makes it worthwhile. I also have a few freelancers working with me when I have larger orders. Working with other people is not always easy. If you start hiring help, you need to plan for training. You need to explain what you want, and how you want it and show them a specific example. People have very different quality standards, and not spelling out expectations has set me up for disappointment numerous times. Old fashioned checklists help. I like working with single moms or women who don't have many sources of income—it is a good thing to be able to help in this difficult economic climate. I let them work out of their houses. I set a price per piece and they work towards a deadline.

Actually, I work with brand new neck tie fabrics. I buy the remnants (the end of the roll) as well as the fabric samples that the tie makers can't use. They are still new and beautiful, but they are too small for them to make a tie. So, it is a win-win situation. And I love the fact that nothing goes to waste!

As to the sourcing... that's one of the trickiest parts. It comes down to cultivation of relationships with the people distributing these remnants (as they are in limited supply), following-up and being polite and very persistent.

The Bay Area is unique in this respect—people try hard to re-use and re-cycle, and there are places/outlets where remnants of all sorts are sold. In Europe it may be a little more difficult but I am sure that calling up the manufacturer could produce the desired results. Just be prepared to take it all—they won't let you have a bag or two. They are more likely to ask you to take a truck-load and free them from the stuff!

My main goal is to establish a broad enough customer base I can rely on, and not necessarily pursue a rapid growth. I don't need to be a large company. I am old-fashioned in this respect—I think that beautiful, exquisite products should not be mass-produced or even hand-produced in large quantities. I am very happy with being small and successful.

It is also important to make a decision about which stores the products should be offered at—my products can be found only at a limited number of stores I deem stylish and high-end enough to sell them.

How did you arrive at the correct price point for your products? Any tips or pricing formulas for other designer/makers to ensure they are making a decent living from their handmade items?

In my case I went to a few expensive stores and looked at what similar quality items are selling for. Don't be afraid to ask for a high price—just make sure the price fits your market. Make sure you know which market you are after and stick to your price. Don't lower the price as a motivation to make them buy.

An important thing though is making sure your web prices and the store prices are more or less consistent. Stores can (and do occasionally) complain that customers can see the product in the store and then buy it on-line cheaper.

Please describe the absolute stand-out best moment for you so far? And the worst?

Getting into Gump's! Gump's is an iconic luxury gift store in San Francisco and has been around for many decades. I called the buyer, made a presentation, incorporated her suggestions into the product and made another presentation. And they bought!

Lows... It sometimes gets very lonely. If you are spending most of your time by yourself, motivation may dwindle. Have people around you—even just honest friends who can look at your work and give you feedback and cheer you up. This is the only part I miss from my corporate life—the team, the people. So, be prepared.

What's the best piece of advice you've been given. What do you wish you'd know back when you started out. Is there anything you would do differently?

I wish there was a list of all good fairs and shows happening in my area with dates, cost, and rating. It took me a long while to compile it and I missed out on a number of shows. Also, I wish I had planned better at the beginning—you need to have stockpiled product before the Holiday rush and be ready to concentrate on selling, not last-minute production. Time flies by quickly.

Also, if possible, always be there in person for your shows. Tell people what you are doing, explain, engage, smile, pull them into your booth from the walk way. After a few hours of walking around buyers can be very tired and distracted. You may need to get their attention in an unconventional way sometimes. Don't outsource the sales role at shows—or at least be present.

What are your hopes and dreams for Paisley and Stripes?

I would like to be established in Texas, Florida, and the Southern States. These are the places where my product would fit best—people dress up, appreciate great craftsmanship and can afford it. I would also like to be able to be fully independent financially—not because it is a necessity, but just for the tickle of it!

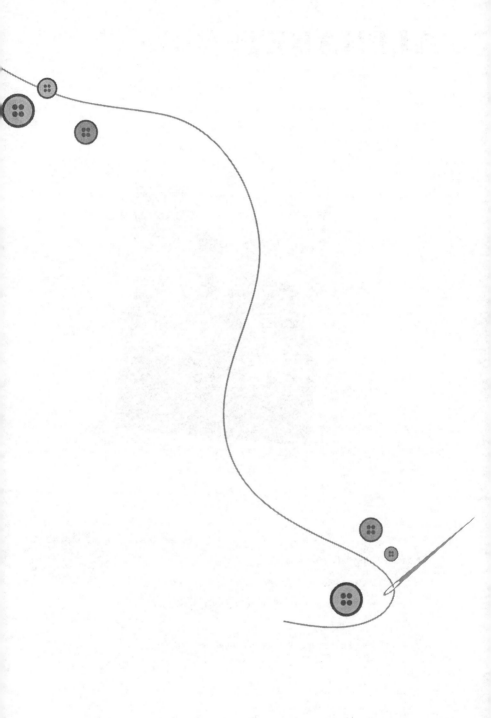

ALPHABETBAGS

Name: **Hayley & Lucas Lepola**

Company Name: **Alphabet Bags / Keep Calm Gallery**

Founded in: **2007 (Keep Calm Gallery) / 2008 (Alphabet Bags)**

Location: **London, UK**

Website: **www.keepcalmgallery.com / www.alphabetbags.com**

Keep Calm Gallery was established in January 2007 by Lucas and Hayley Lepola, now a husband and wife team! The site was born out of their passion for typography in poster design, British heritage and the medium of screen printing.

In the beginning Keep Calm Gallery was run from their university halls. The site is now run from their cosy office in South East London, not far from their small house, which they share with their two handsome cats. The two twenty-somethings studied at University in Birmingham—Hayley has a degree in the History of Art and Lucas has a degree in Business and Management. They share all tasks, from day to day jobs, to the design of new products. All in all they make a pretty good team, although their office Christmas party can be a little quiet!

What started with a few prints from the two of them soon grew into a site featuring a wide selection of work from some fantastic artists, designers and print makers. They work closely with a fantastic group of artists and printers to be able to offer the highest quality fine art prints for the home.

In 2008 Lucas and Hayley launched Keep Calm Gallery's sister site, Alphabet Bags. Alphabet Bags launched quite simply with 26 cotton totes screen printed with the letters A to Z. Since then they have regularly added new collections to Alphabet Bags, from bold typographic designs on their bags, to coin purses, wash bags and travel card holders.

Tell us a bit about what you did before launching Alphabet Bags? Were you both also working regular jobs when you first started out?

We had been running our first website, Keep Calm Gallery (KCG), for about 18 months before launching Alphabet Bags (AB). Luckily everything was going well with KCG so that was a full time job for us both before launching. When we launched KCG I,(Lucas) was in my final year at university and Hayley had recently finished her course at university. I had been studying Business and Management and Hayley History of Art. We didn't have full time jobs at that point, so luckily had some free time in between final year coursework to spend working on getting KCG up and running.

Where did the idea come from? What research did you do before you took plunge?

Launching KCG wasn't a huge leap. We weren't setting out to create a huge business and we didn't have any particularly grand ideas. We were students without much of an income, but with a big interest in prints, posters, screen printing, letterpress, typography and vintage items. Together we collected a lot of prints which we didn't have much room for! We had always been fascinated by the history behind the WW2 'Keep calm and carry on' poster design, and it was the inspiration behind launching the website. It seemed like a good time as it was difficult for Hayley to get work in a gallery due to the amount of experience most required, so starting our own online gallery seemed like a great solution. We knew we wanted to work with artists, work on our own ideas, and show a collection of handmade prints. Our interest in the 'Keep calm and carry on' design seemed like an ideal starting point as we always thought that high quality handmade reproductions of the poster in a variety of colors would just be fantastic and something unique that hadn't been done before. So that's what we started with, and we decided our other ideas would follow if there was interest in these. We didn't do a great deal of research other than to ensure we were working with a fantastic printer and to make sure that our very basic website was tidy, informative and easy to use.

About 18 months later we decided to launch AB. It's difficult to pinpoint exactly where the idea came from! We had a real love for typography, particularly big, bold letters, which we seemed to collect. We had also often spoken about making great quality tote bags, as we found that so many cotton bags out there were so thin and flimsy that they just didn't look great after a few weeks of use, even if they featured lovely designs. One day I think I suggested in the office (which was then at home) "How about bags with initials on them, initial bags, alphabet bags?!" We hadn't come across anything like this before and we wanted one for ourselves! We mocked up some designs and when we saw on screen how we wanted them to look we had a lot of confidence that they could be a great collection. We wanted to launch the brand fairly quickly so the bags would be available in time for Christmas 2008, so we kept the new website very simple and most research was dedicated to finding the best quality cotton and a great manufacturer. We saw a lot of bags! We learned that great manufacturers are hard to come by, but when we found one, we were delighted with the finished product. We did our best to research the popularity of each initial, but it was guesswork at this stage so we just started off with a fairly small number of each letter. We put the bags online and eagerly waited to see the reaction!

When you first started out, what were your aims? How does where you are today differ from those initial ambitions?

For the first year of business we didn't plan more than a few weeks ahead. As a result we didn't have any grand plans or ambitions for the business, which at that time was just KCG. As I was still studying at university and Hayley had found work at an auction house it was a bit of a challenge sometimes juggling between working on the website, thinking about new collections, and devoting enough time to lectures, exams and work. In the long run though I think this was beneficial. As we started off slowly KCG was a hobby which did not require a scary investment and we didn't have to do anything too drastic like ditching studying or a day job in order to give it the amount of attention it required to grow at a speed we were comfortable with.

Our long term aims were just planning new releases a few weeks in advance. We had a bigger focus on short term aims such as providing speedy shipping, attention to detail and great customer service. We knew that these were the things that would be important if we wanted KCG to be around in the future. They were also the things we wanted from other online retailers, important things that unfortunately some were lacking all too often.

In that first year or so whilst still living and working in university halls it was nice to have an additional income from print sales, but working together in creating something we were both interested in and excited about was the best part of the experience at that stage. In the back of our minds we had always hoped to work for ourselves and to have a business which we were passionate about that had the potential to become a family business, something that we could develop in the long term.

Did you do a business plan? How did you raise your start-up capital?

Perhaps we should have written something down, but we didn't have any sort of business plan. At that stage KCG was more of a hobby or a project, something for us to do that gave us the chance to work together, that would be more interesting for us than other part time jobs available to us in our circumstances. We knew our short term plans, but couldn't have made a long term plan at that early stage. If we had done so, I don't know if we would have predicted or aimed to be where we are today! Our start-up capital consisted of about half of one terms student loan, which was spent the day it was received.

For others starting out in business we would recommend making some kind of plan if you do have big ambitions. If you are content with starting out with a small scale project or hobby then it's not unnecessary, but not so important. The early stages are about learning, so plans might change and it's good to be open to new ideas. It's great if you have some savings you can use for capital, without over stretching yourself as there's always the risk you could never see it again. We were lucky to have just enough cash available from a student loan, and if you are a student thinking about starting out in business or investing in an idea then it could work for you too. There are worse things your student loan can be spent on!

All your bags are screen-printed and stitched in the UK. Tell us the challenges you faced finding the right suppliers?!

It was difficult to find a great supplier, particularly one with access to the type of high quality cotton we wanted to use. At the time we didn't have a huge directory of suppliers to approach and at times we didn't feel we were going to be able to find exactly what we wanted. We did eventually, though it took a lot of searching and a lot of calling around requesting samples. We're still working with the same supplier for our bags today though so it was well worth it. We already worked with a great printer for KCG editions, and fortunately they could print our bags to the same standard too. We didn't have to commit to a huge print run for each letter initially, however overall we still ended up with a few thousand bags in our first delivery. Given that we had no idea whether the bags would prove popular it was quite a lot of stock to hold (at the time in our small flat).

From that initial range of 26 bags, you now have tons of other styles and other items (purses, wash bags, tea towels etc.) Was adding each new style a big financial leap? How did you find the right suppliers for each new item?

After our first year running AB we thought it was really important to keep adding to the range, and there were so many collections we wanted to work on. At that stage we didn't have any idea where to find the right suppliers for new collections such as coin purses and wash bags. A collaboration we worked on to produce diamanté initial bags introduced us to working with factories overseas. Following on from this we were able to finally get our coin purses sampled and produced. A little over a year later we began working on our wash bags and card holders, which proved a real challenge at times. Since our first delivery of coin purses we've had several changes of factory to get the quality we are happy with. We're still very much learning about this process.

With these factories the minimum orders have always been much larger so there was a bigger risk involved financially, but with any new collection we've never taken on more than we could manage. The main problem we have encountered is finding enough space for these deliveries when they arrive! On a few occasions a large delivery has prompted us to change our office space or even move altogether.

Please describe the space you work from, and how has this changed from when you started out?

Today we work from an office in a business park in South East London, about a 15 minute drive from where we live. We have a lot of stock to store, particularly in the run up to Christmas, so we recently took on another unit at the business park for additional space. In total we have about 1000 square feet.

It's a big jump from where we started. KCG launched in a tiny room in student halls, before being run from our parent's homes briefly. When we moved in together in London we ran KCG and launched AB from our small first floor flat, with just a tiny home office in the second bedroom and the living room for storing our first delivery of bags. A year later we moved to the house we have lived in for the past three years. For about two years it served as a home and office, but as our collections grew and our first delivery of coin purses arrived we knew that we couldn't realistically work from home any longer. We had storage and stock in every room, and it was becoming very difficult to move!

It was a challenge finding the right office space in South East London. Rent is high and we had some very specific requirements. We had to have a ground floor unit, and needed something that was the right combination of office and light industrial. It was just the two of us working in the space, so it had to be comfortable, but mainly suitable for storing our products. We've no doubt that moving to an office space was a good idea, it was lovely to get the house back so we could really enjoy being at home without tripping over boxes. We have had difficulties with the office at times though, from floods to finding the right insurance policy and difficult neighbors. We've now outgrown the space we are in and are looking to move into a bigger space next year.

So—are two minds really better than one? Are you glad you did this together? Do you think you would have still launched a business had you been single or working alone?

We're definitely glad that we started KCG and AB together, and we feel very lucky to still be working together today after more than five years. Some friends tell us they couldn't ever imagine working with their partner every day, but we have other friends in the same position who think it's a great opportunity if you can do it.

In our case two minds are better than one. We collaborate on everything, exchanging good ideas and recognizing the not-so-good ideas. We're very much on the same wave length which is great for allowing ideas to develop quickly.

We would like to think we would still have started businesses had we not been together, but who knows, perhaps we provided just the encouragement each of us needed to do it.

At what point did you do your first trade show?

We haven't actually attended a trade show to date! It's been on our 'to do' list for quite some time, but we found that in the early stages of the business we concentrated on selling through our websites directly to customers, and as we grew we began to focus on developing our collections and growing our range. As it's just been the two of us here this has taken up so much of our time and trade shows got sidelined.

Through word of mouth and good press coverage we have been lucky enough to be stocked by some great retailers and have developed relationships with some great independents and larger well known retailers. I'm sure we will do a trade show at some point in the future, but it's good to know that they're not the only way to become known by retailers.

Your products have received TONS of press coverage. Did you do all this yourself?

We've been pretty lucky to get some great press coverage both online and offline. We've always managed our own PR for KCG, and for the first year running AB we also handled the PR there. Before we started neither of us had much experience with this side of things, so when approaching magazines and journalists we were very personal and friendly, just sending a hand written letter to introduce us and what we did. I think this served us well and let our brands stand out from other standard press releases.

We pick up a lot of magazines and still hand write a note to stylists, journalists and editors where possible. Bombarding magazines with press releases for everything you do wouldn't work for us in the long run. If you've got something that works for a particular feature that's great, but it's best to develop a good relationship and not to be too overbearing.

We've worked with a PR company for AB for over a year now. We found that we couldn't effectively handle the PR for both AB and KCG in house, and the specialised PR company knew more about opportunities in the fashion and accessories area, which would have likely passed us by. We've had a great relationship with the PR team there, they know exactly what our plans for the brand are and what we would like to achieve. It's important to discuss this in detail with a PR company before beginning to work with them.

Is it still just the two of you running the company? Do you plan to take on any employees, or is this too big a leap right now?

It is still just the two of us here in the office. At very busy times such as Christmas, Hayley's mum Jane very kindly helps us out by packing and posting some orders from her home. When things aren't too busy we can manage as just the two of us. However, sometimes now we find that we're both too busy with the day to day jobs that our new projects and plans are taking a back seat which can be frustrating. This is particularly the case from August through until January. We can feel quite burnt out in the 70 hour weeks in December, but when you know that there are people out there who are interested in what you're doing it really makes it worthwhile.

Sometimes people think that if you're your own boss you can take it easy and work fewer hours but that's really not the case. We've found that in what we do you have to be very disciplined and want to work as much as is needed in order to achieve the things you are aiming for and to be a success.

We will be looking to get some help in the office next year to allow us to spend enough time on planning new collections all year round. It's an unknown for us and something we've put off doing for some time, but we're learning now that it's a necessary step and an important part of our growth. We will have to change the way we work but we're sure that any adjustments will be worthwhile as it will be so important for us to delegate tasks in order to move forward.

Words of wisdom! What do you wish you had known more about when you started out? Anything you would do differently?

A lot of people say it, but you really do learn from your mistakes in business! Given that, there isn't a lot we would change or do differently as it's always important to learn. Perhaps we would have moved into the office sooner, or taken on help sooner, but there haven't been any catastrophic mistakes that have been detrimental to us.

Although when we started out the business worked well as a project or hobby, we probably should have been a little more business-like with our accounting. When we knew the business would be something we wanted to devote ourselves to in the long term, it was difficult to retrospectively tidy up our bookkeeping!

What does the future hold for Alphabet Bags...any exciting plans you'd like to share? Where would you like the company to be 5 years from now?

We have a lot of new ideas in the pipeline for both KCG and AB. Particularly when we have help in the office we will be focusing on adding new collections more regularly. We're also looking forward to website redesigns and some re-branding, which is exciting but also hard work. There will be lots of decisions about small things which will test us and we will find out whether we really are still on the same wavelength! In five years we would be delighted to still be in business together and doing the things we enjoy. If customers are still interested in the things we're introducing then we will feel incredibly lucky. We would still love to be a family business, but with some extra help to lighten the load during the busy periods. We're always considering new ideas, so who knows, by this time we may be working on another brand too!

Hayley & Lucas'
Top Ten Tips for Creative Business Success

1) If you can, start off small and slowly. You'll have less pressure and fewer worries. If you can test your ideas before quitting the day job that's great.

2) Be prepared to work hard and for long hours.

3) Make sure you take a break. Time can fly when you're working hard and have a lot you want to achieve. Remember to stop and recharge every now and then. Some of the best ideas pop into your head when you're away from the office.

4) Ask others for their opinions. You don't need to take on mountains of market research as a small business. If you have friends and family who can be honest with you make sure you run your ideas by them. Their feedback will be valuable.

5) As you grow do your best to delegate. It's valuable to know how to do your bookkeeping and complete a Vat or sales tax return, but in the long run that's going to be very time consuming. If you're spending too much time on the paperwork you will slow down your business' development.

6) Don't underestimate the importance of your suppliers. You need to work with the best suppliers who can reliably deliver exactly what you need. Don't just settle for a supplier, keep looking until you find the right match.

7) Develop good relationships with the press and offer visitors the option to subscribe to a newsletter from day one. Over time your list will grow and become one of the most important methods of letting customers know about what you are doing.

8) If you're online, don't neglect your website. It's incredibly important to make sure it looks good, presents your products clearly and well and is straightforward for customers to use. If you have customers contacting you to compliment the functionality of your website then you've got it right.

9) Enjoy it! You have to really love what you do when you run your own business.

10) None of the above matter much if you don't have excellent customer service. Always be friendly, helpful, grateful and quick to reply. As it's your business and you love what you do these things should come naturally.

QUEEN BEE CREATIONS

Name: **Rebecca Pearcy**

Company Name: **Queen Bee Creations**

Founded in: **1996**

Location: **Portland, Oregon, USA**

No. of Employees: **6**

Website: **www.queenbee-creations.com**

In 1995, Rebecca Pearcy designed a vinyl wallet for herself, which later became the Wonder Wallet, now the Maximo Wallet. That was the beginning of Queen Bee Creations. Queen Bee began selling wholesale to a few boutiques, and now sell to stores in most states in the country, as well as overseas.

Rebecca and her team take pride in sewing and finishing all the products that they sell, and put a tremendous amount of time, care, and creativity into everything they make and do. What began as a little cut-and-paste catalog enterprise has blossomed into a retail and wholesale endeavor that sells unique, handmade accessories to folks worldwide.

Tell us about Queen Bee Creations, the company as it stands today?

Queen Bee has changed a whole lot over the past year. I started off all by myself and over the past 15 years, grew the business to 15 staff members. This year, I changed the business model quite a bit, and became smaller in size. Queen Bee's former production manager spun a business off of QB—she started her own cut and sew manufacturing business and now they make most of Queen Bee's line. I am focusing on design and small-run production. We have expanded our retail store and are always keeping things fresh in the shop. Sometimes something I design gets made and put out in the shop all in the same day! It's really fun and satisfying. I founded QB in Olympia, WA, but now we are located in Portland OR. We design and make bags, wallets, accessories, home goods, and items for babies/families. We have a retail store that fronts our production house, and visitors can see all the action from the shop. It is our way of being transparent and showing people the process, and the people who work hard to create these hand made goods!

What did you do before you launched the company? How did you get the idea for Queen Bee?

I was in college and worked at various small businesses, where I learned how to sew on industrial sewing machines and just a lot about small business in general. I also went to Philadelphia and did an apprenticeship at The Fabric Workshop, where I learned how to design & hand-print pattern in repeat. This planted the seed for what is now the new Rebecca Pearcy Textiles line.

I don't remember a moment when I "got the idea" for Queen Bee. It was really born out of the things I was already doing: buying funky fabric at thrift stores and making clothing, accessories, and more. It was a very organic evolution. Many of my product inspirations just come from needing something for myself and wanting to make it instead of buy it. What is now the Maximo Wallet (previously the Wonder Wallet) was the first item I designed that is still in the line—that was the initial inspiration. I was making and selling things while also working a couple of part time jobs, and as Queen Bee got busier I realized that the only way I would know if I could make a go at my own business is if I worked at it full time. So I quit my jobs and haven't looked back since!

Tell us about the very early days of the company? Were you still working a job?

Yes, I was definitely working other jobs when I started it. I started really small—I was working from a corner of my bedroom and then a spare room in a shared house. Then I realized that it might be a good idea to separate work from home, which was a great move! At the beginning I did everything myself. I started small so it was ok to be doing everything alone, but as Queen Bee grew, I definitely needed assistance.

Can you remember your first sale? And the first store that agreed to stock your products?

I have been selling items that I make for so long (literally since elementary school, but more so in high school and college) that there's no way I can remember the first sale. When I started Queen Bee, there was no internet or email or Etsy or Facebook. I can't even remember how I landed my first wholesale account! I think I just heard about a cool shop in Seattle, so I contacted them and they started carrying the line. It was really exciting to start selling wholesale—I distinctly remember setting the goal of selling in a handful of boutiques, and quickly achieved that goal.

When you first started out, what were your aims?

I didn't set out with really specific goals. Again, it was just a very organic process.
I loved to make things and other people liked what I was making, so it was a natural progression to start selling these items. I didn't know where it would lead me, but I certainly didn't think that I would someday have 15 employees! Both of my parents were/are self employed, so it was an easy thing to envision working for myself, and they have always been so supportive.

Please describe the place you work from today—how does this differ to when you started out?

I am so lucky to work in an amazing space today. Two years ago, we moved into a building on a developing and expanding street in Portland. It's a great neighborhood and we got to design the build out of the renovation to suit our needs. We've always been in drafty old warehouses (which do have their charms), so this has been a major step up. There is a ton of natural light, which is wonderful. And we opened our first official retail store which is designed to give a view into the production areas so that customers and visitors can see the folks that are actively making the items that they are shopping in the store. It's a really unique and cool environment that intends to connect the buyers with the makers.

It was huge to bring on others to help me with the business. It started with a friend volunteering to help me, because he could see that I needed it! I would buy him lunch and he would help me for free. He ended up becoming my business partner for several years! It was a big, scary thing to start to actually pay employees and deal with all the taxes, etc. I tend to want to do everything myself (a dangerously common thing with creative people!) but I highly recommend finding a good bookkeeper, accountant, attorney, and business counselor to help with the things that really should be done right.

It's pretty easy to tell when you need to get help with making the items—when you just can't keep up with demand or you're having to turn down business that you would like to take but you just don't have the capacity. I have just followed the signs I see my business giving to me, while also trying to anticipate and plan for the future. Otherwise there's just a lot of reacting and putting out fires.

For many years we did very little outreach to gain new wholesale accounts. We didn't advertise and we didn't attend trade shows. We grew by word of mouth and our product advertised itself. This was a very fortunate position to be in as we didn't have to spend the resources to bring business our way, and we were growing plenty fast. A few years ago we decided to start advertising more and also began showing at trade shows. Trade shows can be such a mixed bag—it is a lot of work and expensive to try them out and see which ones are the right market for your business. They're very expensive and if you don't get many orders you can lose money. We always viewed them as an opportunity to not only get new accounts and orders, but also build relationships. That said, we did discontinue attending shows when we just couldn't justify the expense and also chose to focus more on retail than wholesale.

Chickpea Baby came out of noticing that there weren't many good looking diaper bags out on the market. Some of our customers were already using our Queen Bee Trucker bag as a diaper bag. I saw an opportunity to offer something that the market wasn't fulfilling, which was an easy fit since we were already making bags. Also, I started to be the age when friends and family around my age were starting families. Rebecca Pearcy Textiles has been a line a long time in the making— originally inspired by my apprenticeship at The Fabric Workshop and also just my love of color and bold print on fabrics. And also inspired by buying my first home and making things to decorate it.

You are based in Portland, Oregon, which seems to be a real hub of creative businesses and designer makers. Do you network in the crafty community?

Portland is amazing! And yes, I network, as much as I can, given my busy life. It has been crucial for me to connect with other like-minded folks about business, creativity, life. I really reached out when I was pregnant with my son. I was trying to understand how it might work to balance a small business with being a new mama, so I reached out to other mama small business owners to ask them about their experiences. That was really great. I love talking shop with other business owners—we all deal with many of the same challenges and issues, and it is really unique to be self-employed, so I find those connections to be really valuable. I also have a business counselor who I have been working with for many years—she has helped me navigate so many crossroads, and has helped direct me when I have been unsure of how to proceed and manage.

Cashflow—the main problem with most small businesses! How did you finance the growth of your business?

Ah, cash flow. So hard! We were lucky and for a long time did not have to find money to help finance our growth. But a few years ago we did go into debt for the first time. I am pretty debt-averse, so it was hard to do, but it is ok and very normal and expected for businesses to have to borrow money to make the cash flow. Because of the rough economy over the past few years, it has been hard to pay that debt down, which is frustrating. I have definitely had many scary moments with cash flow and payroll, though I have never, ever, not paid an employee or written a paycheck that has bounced. It is my responsibility to make sure I can manage the money that I have promised to vendors and employees. So if times are hard, I am the one that has taken the hit.

All of your goods are made by hand in Portland. Surely you could achieve higher profit margins if you outsourced production or sent it overseas? How important is it to you to keep production local?

It is essential to me to have our products made local—I have built my business on this foundation, it is part of our brand, and something I am really proud of. Even now, with most of our line being produced by Spooltown, it is all still being made on-site, and our new business model is only creating opportunities for even more goods to be made locally. Luckily there is a lot of support in Portland for locally-made goods, so we are in a good place.

What's the best piece of advice you've been given. Any advice for others thinking of doing their own thing?

Delegate as soon as you can. It is natural for a new small business owner to do everything themselves. But you will burn out and you can't be good at everything. It is hard and scary and sometimes you don't know how to make the money work, but it is really important to create a situation where you get to do the thing only YOU can do—and pay someone else to do the other things. Otherwise you will find that you hardly ever get to do the essential part of your job, whatever it is. I wish I had learned this a lot sooner.

What are your hopes and dreams for Queen Bee? Where would you like the business to be in 5 years time?

I'm interested in continuing to expand the textiles line and collaborate with other folks to produce new ideas. I'd love to get to the point where I can have yardage of my fabric designs printed for me—then I could even sell the fabric which would be fun! And I love working with new fabrics, so I'd like to continue doing that. It is hard to know where it will lead—at the heart of it I would just like to continue being able to follow my inspiration, whatever that is.

Rebecca's
Top Ten Tips for Creative Business Success

1) Take breaks.

2) Connect with other people that are involved in a similar enterprise.

3) Delegate, delegate, delegate.

4) Make sure your pricing is structured so that you are actually making money!

5) Hire people that are better at their job than you are at their job.

6) Make sure you are focusing on what only you can do—and pay others to do the rest.

7) Love what you do! Otherwise it's just too much hard work.

8) Remember that this is YOURS. You are the decider. That doesn't mean that everything is in your control. It does mean that you have a lot of freedom to create your reality and environment.

9) If something isn't working, change it.

10) Be genuine, it will show and the world will respond.

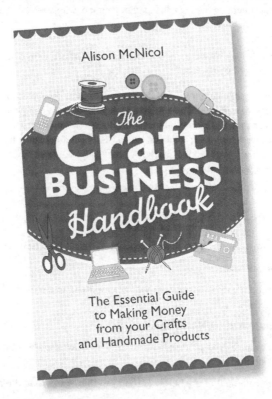

The Etsy Business Handbook:

How To Make Money Selling Your Crafts and Handmade Products In The Online Marketplace

With sales of over $300 million per year, and over 7 million registered users, Etsy is the online marketplace for crafty entrepreneurs.

This book is an essential tool for any crafter aiming to make money online.

Learn how to build and launch a successful Etsy store, take tips from the experts on how to make your products stand out from the crowd, and get ready to generate sales from customers around the world.

Essential reading for any Crafty Entrepreneur!

Search under: The Etsy Handbook / ISBN: 978-1-908707-03-1

www.kyle-craig.com

Do you have a craft business idea?

Would you like to sell the products you make? Start with a great logo, business cards and a website and you could soon be turning your creative dreams into reality!

Approaching a designer doesn't have to be scary or expensive and can really help get your new business up and running. Seeing your scribbled ideas transform into finished graphics is often the first time you really start to feel like a 'business' and with ongoing support and advice, the great little design company can help your new business fly.

Logos • Stationery • Websites • Flyers • Brochures • Adverts Banners • Packaging • Labels • Book design • Illustration

For all enquiries please email
julie@thegreatlittledesigncompany.com
www.thegreatlittledesigncompany.com

Acknowledgements

I hope you enjoyed reading these interviews as much as I enjoyed doing them!

This book wouldn't have been possible without the hard work and generosity of all those crafty entrepreneurs who agreed to be featured. So a big **THANK YOU** to all of you!

Perhaps reading their stories has helped inspire you to take the leap yourself—and if so, I wish you lots of love and luck in taking those next steps towards fulfilling your creative dreams.

I was inspired to write this book—and my other book *The Craft Business Handbook*—by all the many people I met along the way during my own travels in crafty entrepreneurship.

If you do decide to start your own creative business, please keep in touch and let me know how you're getting on!

I've set up a great online community where all we crafty entrepreneurs can meet up to swap tips, share knowledge, offer advice and support each other!

I'll see you there!

Alison xx

The Craft Business Community

...where Crafty Entrepreneurs come together!

Join Us Now For:

Resources – Support – Community
Networking – Inspiration

www.craftbusinesscommunity.com

 The Craft Business Community
 @CraftyBiz